A Taste of the Canadian Rockies

by Myriam Leighton and Chip Olver

▼

Publication Information

Altitude Publishing Canada Ltd.
The Canadian Rockies
1500 Railway Avenue
Canmore, Alberta Canada T1W 1P6

10 9 8 7 6 5 4

Canadian Cataloguing in Publication Data
Includes index
ISBN 1-55153-031-7
1. Cookery—Rocky Mountains, Canadian (B.C. and Alberta) 2. Cookery, Canadian—Alberta style I.Olver, Chip, 1955– II. Leighton, Myriam, 1962–
TX715.6T37 1994   641.597123'3   C94-910697-6

Made in Western Canada
Printed and bound in Western Canada by Friesen Printers

Altitude GreenTree Program

 Altitude Publishing will plant in Western Canada twice as many trees as were used in the manufacturing of this product.

Design and page layout: Stephen Hutchings

Front cover photograph: Banff from Sulphur Mountain, *Douglas Leighton*

▼

Contents

Introduction   **5**

Appetizers, Sauces and Special Dressings   **7**

Soups and Salads   **31**

Entreés   **61**

Desserts and Breakfasts   **111**

Recipes in the Canadian Rockies   **149**

Credits   **150**

Restaurant Listing   **151**

Index   **155**

▲

Banff Avenue and Cascade Mountain, 1887

▼

Introduction and Acknowledgments

A Taste of The Canadian Rockies includes mouth-watering recipes from restaurants in the town's of Banff, Jasper, Lake Louise, Waterton and Canmore as well as selections from the resorts and back country lodges that are nestled throughout the Canadian Rockies. Some distinguishing characteristics of tourist destinations are the incredible variety of dining opportunities, the outstanding quality offered in the restaurants and chefs who come from around the world to create dishes to tempt you and your friends.

You can imagine how difficult it was to select the eating establishments and recipes that are represented in this collection. (At last count the town of Banff alone had more than 70 restaurant listings in the phone book.) We started with our own favourites, asked others what their favourites were and then combined the lists.

The original version of this Canadian best seller was published in 1985 as *A Taste of Banff*. We realized your visit to the Canadian Rockies includes other locations you'd like memories of and so expanded the book to give you just that.

Warm thanks to:

• **Doug Leighton**, for the original book idea, for the spectacular colour photographs throughout the book and for his support,

• **Jim, Jamie and Linda Olver** for their support,

• **the chefs and restaurant owners** who made this book possible and who supplied their favourite recipes for you to recreate at home,

• **Pat Zawada and Kathie and Wendy Oakden** for proof reading help,

• **Stephen Hutchings** for giving us the opportunity to realize this project.

We are delighted to present this book for your enjoyment. Now that it is done we are anxious to get into our own kitchens to try out more of these wonderful dishes and impress family and friends!

Cheers and happy dining,

Myriam Leighton and Chip Olver

Baker with display board, *Byron Harmon photograph*, 1923

Appetizers, Sauces and Special Dressings

▼

SPINACH AND CAMBOZOLA CHEESE WRAPPED IN PHYLLO WITH FRESH FRUIT SALSA

serves four

Fresh spinach, washed	8 oz.	250 g
Large white onion, sliced thin	1	1
Unsalted butter	2 tbsp.	30 ml
Salt	to taste	to taste
Ground white pepper	to taste	to taste
Curry powder	pinch	pinch
Cambozola cheese	8 oz.	250 g
Phyllo dough	4 sheets	4 sheets

Melted butter, as needed

Sweat the onion in a saucepan with the butter. When onion is translucent add washed spinach, salt, pepper and curry powder. Cook spinach completely until vibrant green. Cut Cambozola into 4 even slices.

Note: The next few steps need to be done quickly so go over method beforehand. Take each sheet of phyllo dough and lay out on the counter. Brush two of the sheets completely with melted butter, cover each of these sheets with the remaining dough to make a second layer. Brush second layer very lightly with more melted butter.

Cut the two buttered phyllo pieces in half widthwise so there are 4 equal pieces left. Divide cooked spinach into 4 portions. Place each spinach portion at the end of each phyllo piece, place each piece of cheese onto the spinach.

Fold side edges of phyllo up onto the cheese and spinach. (This is so the cheese doesn't ooze out when cooking.) Brush the folded edges with melted butter and proceed to roll up the cheese and spinach in the dough very loosely.

Place cheese bundles onto a baking tray with the seam side down so dough

▲

▼

doesn't unwrap when baked. Bake for 5 to 7 minutes at 375°F(190°C) until golden brown. Spoon fresh fruit salsa (recipe follows) over each one when served. Serve piping hot.

Fresh Fruit Salsa

Strawberries	**2 - 3**	**2 - 3**
Honeydew melon	**1/2**	**1/2**
Cantaloupe melon	**1/2**	**1/2**
Kiwi fruit	**1**	**1**
Fresh pineapple	**1/4**	**1/4**
Mango or papaya	**1**	**1**
Cilantro, chopped	**2 tbsp.**	**30 ml**
Mint, chopped	**2 tbsp.**	**30 ml**

Dice all of the fruit into 1/4" (5 mm) pieces and mix in a bowl. Add chopped cilantro and mint. Option: You can add some zip to this salsa, just add some diced jalapeño pepper. Set salsa aside. Salsa can be made a day ahead if needed.

Lara Christie, Executive Chef
Deer Lodge, Lake Louise

"We are entering the defiles of the Rocky Mountains by the Athabaska River, the woods of Pine are stunted, full of Branches to the ground, and the Aspin, Willow, not much better; strange to say, there is a strong belief that the haunt of the Mammoth, is about this defile, I questioned several, none could positively say, they had seen him, but their belief I found firm and not to be shaken."

David Thompson, explorer, January 5th, 1811 from *Jasper National Park* by M.B. Williams, 1928

▲

▼

SMOKED TROUT CROSTINI

serves four

Smoked trout fillets (skinless, boneless)	8 oz.	250g
Plain yogurt	1/2 cup	125 ml
Mayonnaise	1/4 cup	50 ml
Fresh lemon juice	1 tsp.	5 ml
Fresh dill, chopped very fine	1 tbsp.	15 ml
Onion, minced	2 tbsp.	30 ml
Freshly ground black pepper	to taste	to taste
Salt	to taste	to taste

Place all ingredients in a food processor and purée until you reach a smooth consistency. Cover mixture and refrigerate for 3 to 4 hours.

Crostini

French baguette bread	1	1
Fresh basil, minced	2 tbsp.	30 ml
Garlic, minced	1 tbsp.	15 ml
Parsley, chopped	1 tbsp.	15 ml
Unsalted butter, melted	1/4 cup	125 ml

Cut baguette into 1/2 inch slices diagonally and place on baking sheet. In a bowl mix the basil, melted butter, garlic and chopped parsley. Brush both sides of the bread slices with the mixture. Bake in a 300°F (150°C) preheated oven, occasionally turning over the crostini until they become toasted golden brown. Set aside to cool. Spread each crostini with the smoked trout mixture, garnish with a sprig of fresh dill and serve.

Milos Moravcik, Executive Chef
Inns of Banff Park, Banff

▲

▼

GARLIC HERB SOUFFLÉ

serves six

Garlic cloves, peeled, finely chopped	**6**	**6**
Onion, finely chopped	**2 tbsp.**	**30 ml**
Olive oil, as needed		
Thick béchamel sauce	**1 1/2 cup**	**375 ml**
Mixed fresh herbs, finely chopped	**3 tbsp.**	**45 ml**
Salt and pepper	**to taste**	**to taste**
Eggs, separated	**4**	**4**

Butter & flour, to coat baking dishes

Butter and flour 6 individual soufflé dishes.

Lightly sauté garlic and onion in olive oil - do not brown. In a medium sized mixing bowl, mix together béchamel sauce, sautéed garlic and onion, fresh herbs, salt and pepper. Add egg yolks and mix well. Whisk egg whites until stiff. Fold into egg yolk mixture. Fill soufflé dishes and bake immediately for 20 minutes in a preheated 400°F (200°C) oven or until puffed and firm in the middle.

Serve immediately.

Scott Schroeder, Executive Chef
Lake O'Hara Lodge, Yoho National Park

"'What is life?' asked the wise looking man in spectacles.

'Two weeks in Banff', said the Calgary girl, 'that's life for me.'"

Banff Crag and Canyon, August 20, 1904

▼

QUESADILLA WITH HOT ITALIAN SAUSAGE AND AVOCADO SALSA

serves four

Hot Italian sausage	8 oz.	250 g
Flour tortillas	4	4
Monterey Jack cheese, shredded	2 cups	500 ml
Mild cheddar cheese, shredded	1 cup	250 ml
Italian sun dried tomatoes in olive oil	1/2 cup	125 ml
Jalapeño peppers, chopped fine	2 tbsp.	30 ml
Chives, chopped fine	1/2 cup	125 ml

Remove Italian sausage from casing and fry in a skillet until cooked, set aside.

Lay the tortillas flat on a cookie sheet, distribute the cheese equally among the tortillas making sure to cover the entire areas except for a 1/4" (5 mm) from the border. Remove sun dried tomatoes from olive oil, pat dry and chop fine. Distribute the Italian sausage, sun dried tomatoes, jalapeño and chives equally over the tortillas.

Place cookie sheet in the oven at 375°F (190°C) and bake just until the cheese has melted, approximately 8 to 10 minutes. Remove from the oven and fold over each quesadilla, cut each into 4 pieces and serve with Avocado Salsa and a dollop of sour cream.

Avocado Salsa

(makes approximately three cups)

Avocados, peeled, seeded, diced	2	2
Tomatoes, seeded and diced	1/2 cup	125 ml
Cilantro, chopped fine	1/4 cup	50 ml
Red onion, diced	3 tbsp.	45 ml
Garlic clove, minced	1	1
Fresh lime juice	1 tbsp.	15 ml

▲

▼

Jalapeño peppers, seeded &
  diced ....1 tsp.......5 ml
Coarse salt ....1 tsp.......5 ml
Fresh ground black pepper ....1/8 tsp. ..1 ml

Place all ingredients in a bowl and mix gently. Salsa tastes best on the day it is prepared.

Milos Moravcik, Executive Chef
Inns of Banff Park, Banff

HOT ARTICHOKE, CHEDDAR AND CRAB DIP

serves four
Artichoke hearts, drained ....1 can......1 can
Mayonnaise ....2/3 cup ..150 ml
Sour cream ....2/3 cup ..150 ml
Parmesan cheese............................2/3 cup ..150 ml
Crab meat.....................................1/4 cup ..50 ml
Dried tarragon ....1 tbsp.....15 ml
Cheddar cheese, shredded................1/2 cup ..125 ml

Chop artichokes and mix well with mayonnaise, sour cream, parmesan, crab meat and tarragon. Bake in earthenware dish topped with cheddar in pre-heated 440°F (220°C) oven until bubbling. Serve with crudities such as nacho chips, carrot sticks or fennel, etc.

Dave Husereau, Chef de Cuisine
Fiddle River Seafood Company, Jasper

▲

▼

BUFFALO SATAY

serves four to six

Marinade

Hoisin sauce	1 cup	500 ml
Plum sauce	6 tbsp.	90 ml
Rice vinegar	1/2 cup	125 ml
Honey	2 tbsp.	30 ml
Dry sherry	2 tbsp.	30 ml
Chinese chili sauce	1 tbsp.	15 ml
Garlic cloves, chopped	2 to 4	2 to 4
Green onions, chopped	2	2
Coriander seed	1 tbsp.	15 ml

Mix marinade ingredients.

Meat

Buffalo meat	1 lb.	500 g

Slice meat into very thin strips and ribbon on to a bamboo skewer. Place in marinade 24 hours or more. Grill on barbecue or cook under broiler. Serve with dipping sauce.

Variation: Can be made with beef, chicken or pork.

Dipping Sauce

Peanuts, chopped	1/4 cup	50 ml
Lime juice	2 tbsp.	30 ml
Green onion, minced	2	2
Garlic cloves, chopped	2	2
Coconut milk	3/4 cup	175 ml
Peanut butter	4 tbsp.	60 ml

▲

▼

Dark soya sauce	1 tbsp.	15 ml
Brown sugar	1 tbsp.	15 ml
Cumin	1 tsp.	2 ml
Coriander seed	1 1/2 tsp.	7 ml
Chinese chili sauce	1 tbsp.	15 ml

Mix all ingredients together.

Tom Hayes, Executive Chef
Buffalo Mountain Lodge, Banff

DELICIOUS CHEESE ROLLS (TIROPETA)

serves twelve to fourteen

Eggs, separated	6	6
Feta cheese, crumbled	2 cups	500 ml
Cottage cheese	2 cups	500 ml
Blue cheese (optional)	1/2 cup	125 ml
Phyllo	2 lb.	1 kg
Butter, melted	1 lb.	500 g

Beat egg yolks, add feta cheese, mix well. Add cottage cheese and blue cheese, mix well. Fold in stiffly beaten egg whites. Cut phyllo sheets in halves or thirds, brush with hot melted butter. Place 1 teaspoonful (5 ml) of cheese mixture in the bottom centre of phyllo. Fold over 1/3 on each side, brush with hot melted butter. Roll up as for jelly roll. Place on cookie sheet. Bake in 350°F (180°C) preheated oven for 15 minutes or until done.

Tom and Maria Lambropoulos, Owners
Balkan, The Greek Restaurant, Banff

▼

CILANTRO CHILI MAYONNAISE

makes three cups (750 ml)

Cilantro, chopped	1 cup	250 ml
Garlic gloves	8	8
Jalapeño peppers	2	2
Ground cumin	4 tsp.	20 ml
Mayonnaise	2 cups	500 ml

In a food processor or blender, purée the cilantro, garlic, chilies and cumin. Stir into the mayonnaise.

May be refrigerated. Great for perking up sandwiches, burgers or for a vegetable dip.

If you think this will be too spicy for your tastes you can calm it down by removing the seeds from the Jalapeño chilies.

Kim Purdy
Coyote's Deli & Grill, Banff

"The Canadian Pacific Railway ought to have a commission on detective cameras, kodaks, hawkeyes, etc.... Whenever you stop at a station, all the steps for getting down are packed with people taking pot shots with kodaks. American children learn kodaking long before they learn to behave themselves.... every operator imagines he is going to kodak an Indian; but the wily Indian sits in the shade, where instantaneous photography availeth not, and, if he observes himself being 'time-exposed' covers his head with a blanket."

Douglas Sladen, 1895, in On the Cars and Off

▲

**Three Sisters Mountain
near Canmore, Alberta**

▼

SKOKI HEALTH BREAD

makes four loaves

Bread

Warm water	4 1/2cups	.1125 ml
Oil	1/2 cup	..125 ml
Honey	1/2 cup	..125 ml
Molasses	1/2 cup	..125 ml
Salt	5 tsp	......25 ml
Whole wheat flour	4 cups	....1 l
Sesame seeds	1/4 cup	..50 ml
Millet seeds	1/4 cup	..50 ml
Poppy seeds	1/4 cup	..50 ml
Yeast	4 tsp	......20 ml
Baker's flour	8 cups	....2 l

Glaze (optional)

Egg, beaten
Poppy seeds, as needed

Combine all the ingredients in a large bowl. Add enough flour to make a kneadable ball, then knead for 10 minutes or more until dough is like a baby's bottom. Let rise until doubled in bulk. Punch down, knead into flour loaves and let rise in the loaf pans for about 40 minutes. Bake until hollow sounding when tapped.

To glaze, when dough is in pans, paint with egg before second rising. Shake poppy seeds over tops.

Skoki Lodge, Banff National Park

▲

▼

BAKED GOAT CHEESE WRAPPED IN PHYLLO PASTRY

serves two

Mild goat cheese	7 oz.	200g
Phyllo pastry	1 sheet	1 sheet
Medium red bell pepper, roasted, diced	1	1
Clarified butter	1/2 lb.	250g

Cut phyllo in half, brush with clarified butter on outer edges. Place half the goat cheese on each of the phyllo sheets. Place the diced pepper over the goat cheese. Fold each of the sides over the goat cheese. Brush the finished product with clarified butter. Bake in a 350°F (180°C) preheated oven for 15 minutes or until brown. Serve with salsa.

Salsa

Medium tomato, peeled, seeded	1	1
Onion	1/2	1/2
Garlic clove, minced	to taste	to taste
Tabasco	splash	splash
Worcestershire sauce	splash	splash
Thyme	pinch	pinch
Basil	pinch	pinch
Oregano	pinch	pinch
Lemon juice	pinch	pinch

Combine all the salsa ingredients and allow to sit refrigerated for a couple of hours.

Aaron Cundliffe, Executive Chef
Emerald Lake Lodge, Yoho National Park

▲

▼

TICINO MARINATED SALMON

for one side of salmon

Side of fresh salmon	1-1 1/2 lb.	500-750g
Brown sugar	2 cups	500 g
White peppercorns, crushed	1/4 cup	50 ml
Allspice, crushed	1/4 cup	50 ml
Salt or rock salt	1/2 cup	125 ml
Liquid smoke	1 tbsp.	15 ml
Fresh dill, chopped	2 oz.	55 g

Combine all ingredients except the dill, pat the mixture over the salmon (skin down). Place dill on top and marinate (covered) in the refrigerator for 3 days.

After 3 days take marinade off and strain. The liquid from marinade can be mixed with 1 tsp. (5 ml) Dijon mustard and a little Pernod. Brush on slices as you serve salmon. Or marinade can be mixed with fresh dill and sour cream as a dip.

Salmon can also be served warm in portions as you heat it in the oven at 350°F (180°C) for approximately 10 minutes.

Markus Wespi, Chef/Co-owner
Ticino Restaurant, Banff

"The Rocky Mountain Bighorn soon may become milady's latest pet...the tamed sheep...can be taught little tricks...and not only do them for the caretaker but for any visitor. All folks look alike to sheep, once tamed."

Banff Crag and Canyon, May 25, 1928

▼

BROILED SHRIMP WITH AN ASIAN SAUCE

serves four

Asian Sauce

Sunflower seeds, roasted	1/2 cup	125 ml
White garlic cloves	3	3
Soya sauce	1/4 cup	50 ml
White vinegar	1/4 cup	50 ml
Water	1/4 cup	50 ml
Tabasco	3 drops	3 drops
Worcestershire	3 drops	3 drops
Sesame seed oil	1 tbsp.	15 ml
Olive oil	1 tbsp.	15 ml
Cayenne	pinch	pinch
Fresh ground black pepper	to taste	to taste

With a food processor, grind the sunflower seeds and garlic. Add the remaining ingredients and blend well. Refrigerate and stir well before serving.

Broiled Shrimp

Shrimp	20	20
Bamboo skewers	4	4
Olive oil and lemon juice, mixed (each)	3 tbsp.	45 ml
Fresh ground black pepper	to taste	to taste
Lemon wedge or crown garnish	4	4
Parsley sprig	4	4
Sesame seeds, roasted	2 tbsp.	30 ml

▲

▼

Peel, devein and rinse shrimp in cold water. Pat dry with a cloth. Put 5 shrimp on each skewer and dip in olive oil/lemon mixture. Cook on a pre-heated broiler or barbecue - 2 minutes on each side. Season with black pepper.

While the shrimp are cooking, garnish 4 plates. Place cooked skewered shrimp on the dressing. Sprinkle with sesame seeds and serve.

At the Baker Creek Bistro, we have used the Asian Sauce with smoked lamb, lobster, chicken wings and avocado salad. Surely you will discover other items to use it with.

Daniel Martineau, Chef/Partner
Baker Creek Bistro, Lake Louise

"Mr. Helm...became hopelessly lost...when found, he was or seemed to be, partly delirious, keeping up a strange conversation about a lot of mermaids he saw...through a large hole in a rock...We all know Mr. Helm is of sound mind...(and) it was some days before...the mystery was cleared...eight ladies who were bathing in the Cave, complained of a nasty, bold man watching them sporting in the waters of life.

Mr. Helm was never a confirmed bachelor...and now carries a set of opera glasses and swears that next time he will not be fooled easily."

Banff Crag and Canyon, July 26, 1902

▼

BAKED CAMEMBERT

per serving
Puff pastry
Camembert..................................3 oz. ......70 g

Roll the puff pastry to a size of 4 x 4 " (10 x 10 cm). Place the Camembert onto one half of the dough, egg wash the edges before folding over. Egg wash the outside and bake at 400°F (200°C) for 5 to 10 minutes until lightly browned.

Mustard sauce

Butter...1 tsp.......5 ml
Coarse mustard ....1 tsp.......5 ml
Dijon mustard..............................1 tsp.......5 ml
Garlic ....1/2 tsp. ..2 ml
Shallots..1/2 tsp. ..2 ml
White wine ....1/3 cup ..75 ml
Whipping cream..........................2/3 cup ..150 ml

Heat butter in a small pan. Add garlic, shallots and mustard (both). Add the white wine and reduce by half. Add the cream and reduce again 2 to 3 minutes (to your liking). Pour sauce on a plate and place baked Camembert in middle. Garnish with a parsley sprig and serve.

Claude Harvey, Chef de Cuisine
Joshua's Restaurant, Banff

"A number of tourists made the discovery on Friday that showers in Banff contain considerable wetness."

Banff Crag and Canyon, July 29, 1901

▼

MUSSELS WITH SAFFRON SAUCE

per serving

Mussels, medium size	12 - 15	12 - 15
White wine	2/3 cup	150 ml
Garlic, minced	2 tsp	10 ml
Shallots	2 tsp	10 ml

Place the mussels in a skillet, add the wine, garlic and shallots. Cover and cook on high burner for 3 to 4 minutes.

Remove the mussels from the skillet. Keep the wine and garlic to finish the sauce.

Saffron Sauce

Saffron	pinch	pinch
Whipping cream	1/2 cup	125 ml
Parmesan cheese	2 tbsp	30 ml

**Julienne of: celery
  carrots, leeks, green and
  red peppers**

With the wine and garlic mix, add saffron, cream, parmesan cheese and julienne. Reduce to desired consistency. Add the mussels with the sauce and serve.

Claude Harvey, Chef de Cuisine
Joshua's Restaurant, Banff

"Oh! she's a hefty feeder, is the mountain climbing girl!"

**from anonymous poem, 'The Mountain Climbing Girl,', Banff
Crag and Canyon, December 15, 1900**

▲

▼

SHANGHAI SHRIMP

serves two

Shrimp, raw and headless

26 to 30 count	16	16
Vegetable oil	1-2 tbsp.	15 to 30 ml
Fresh ginger, peeled and thinly sliced	3 tbsp.	45 ml
Green onions, diced	3 tbsp.	45 ml
Dry sherry	2 tbsp.	30 ml
Soya sauce	2 tbsp.	30 ml
Sugar	2 tsp.	10 ml
Wine vinegar	1/2 tsp.	2 ml

Remove the shell of shrimp except for the tail and last section. Devein. Heat the pan and stir fry the ginger and onions over low heat for 30 seconds, until there is an aroma. Add the shrimp and stir fry over high heat for 1 minute. Add remaining ingredients and stir fry until sauce is glazed for about 2 minutes.

Serving suggestion: Serve as an appetizer with fresh baked sourdough bread to dip in sauce. Sprinkle with chopped fresh parsley just before serving.

Henry Vultier, Executive Chef
Banff Park Lodge, Banff

"Once again the Mounted Police are on the job in Banff and everybody is tickled...Banff citizens may now go to bed and snore as hard as they please."

Banff Crag and Canyon, July 28, 1917

▼

VEGETARIAN BURRITO

makes four

Tortilla shells	4 large	4 large
Refried beans, heated	16 oz can	454 g can
Cheddar, grated	1/2 cup	125 ml
Green onion, sliced	1/4 cup	50 ml
Sour cream	1/2 cup	125 ml
Salsa	1/2 cup	125 ml
Vegetarian Chili, heated	2 cups	500 ml

Spread filling evenly over warm tortilla shells and fold. See Vegetarian Chili recipe on pg 101.

Rudi Thoni, Chef
Papa Georges Restaurant, Jasper

"While the Athabaska Depot was being built, Moberly worked his way down the valley and by Christmas was camped at Fiddle Creek. He has left an interesting description on his fare in Jasper on Christmas Day:

I paid a visit on Christmas Eve to the survey camp, to have a talk and smoke with the staff, some of whom were bewailing the loss of a dinner on the following day, so I invited them down to partake of the luxuries in my camp, about two miles away. My stores consisted at that time of some pemmican, flour and tea, without sugar. I had several courses prepared, the first being pemmican raw, the second pemmican boiled, and in due season the dessert, which was pemmican fried; and my guests looked somewhat disappointed when I informed them they saw all the luxuries before them, and the only thing we could do was to have a good smoke, as I had plenty of tobacco, and try to keep warm."

From *Pack Saddles to Tete Jaune Cache* by James MacGregor

▲

▼

FRESH SCALLOPS WITH BEET AND RED CABBAGE SAUCE

serves six

Butter or margarine	4 tsp.	20 g
Fresh scallops	18	18
Caviar	1 tsp.	5 ml
Salt and pepper	to taste	to taste

Melt the butter, add the scallops and sauté without color, season lightly with salt and pepper.

The Sauce

Butter	4 tsp.	20 g
Onions, chopped	2 tsp.	10 g
Beets, chopped	2 tbsp.	30 g
Red cabbage, chopped	2 tbsp.	30 g
White wine	1/4 cup	50 ml
Fish velouté	1 cup	250 ml
Whipping cream	2 tbsp.	30 ml
Beet brunoise	1 oz.	25 g
Baby beets, cooked	6	6

Melt the butter, add the onions and sauté lightly before adding the red cabbage and the chopped beets, sauté together for about 3 minutes and deglaze with the white wine, reduce until almost all the wine is gone. Add the fish velouté, bring to a boil and simmer slowly for approximately 5 minutes, put in the blender and then through a fine sieve. Bring back to a boil and add the beet brunoise and the cream, simmer for 3 minutes and add salt and pepper to your taste.

To serve: Mirror the sauce on a plate, place 3 scallops in middle and top them with a few grains of caviar. Garnish each plate with a baby beet.

▲

(Brunoise means to finely dice, about 1/8" (3 mm))

Gerhard Frey, Executive Chef
Mount Royal Hotel, Banff

VEAL TORTELLINI WITH SHRIMP CREAM HERB SAUCE

per serving

Veal tortellini, blanched	3 1/2 oz.	100 g
Shrimp, cooked	2 oz.	50 g
Cream herb sauce	1/2 cup	100 ml

Cream herb sauce

Garlic clove, crushed	1	1
Onion, diced	1 oz.	30 g
Chopped fresh herbs (basil, chives, parsley, oregano)	1 oz.	30 g
Whipping cream	3 oz.	85 g
Parmesan cheese	to taste	to taste
Dry white wine	1 oz.	30 g

For sauce, sauté onions and garlic in a little butter or olive oil until tender. Add white wine and cream and bring to a boil, reduce until thickened. Finish by adding grated Parmesan and fresh herbs, season with salt and pepper. Heat pasta in a steamer and toss with butter, salt and pepper. Scoop pasta onto plate, add shrimp and ladle on sauce. Sprinkle with parmesan and fresh herbs.

Kevin Dundon, Executive Chef
Lodge at Kananaskis/Hotel Kananaskis, Kananaskis

TIGER PRAWNS

per serving
Large tiger prawns, peeled
and deveined ....6.............6
Olive oil...1 tbsp.....30 ml
Lemon...1/2 ....1/2
Garlic cloves, chopped ....2.............2
Sprig of rosemary.............................1.............1
Paprika..pinch .....pinch
Cumin seed....................................to taste...to taste
Coriander, ground...........................to taste...to taste
Cilantro, chopped ....to taste...to taste
Fresh ground pepper.......................to taste...to taste

Marinate the prawns in olive oil, garlic, paprika, cumin, coriander and rosemary for 12 hours. Place the prawns in a hot frying pan and sauté 1 minute. Finish with a squeeze of fresh lemon juice and chopped cilantro. Top with ground pepper and serve.

Kevin Dundon, Executive Chef
Lodge at Kananaskis/Hotel Kananaskis, Kananaskis

"One kind of hypocrite is the man who, after thanking the Lord for his dinner, proceeds to find fault with the cook."

Bob Edwards' Summer Annual, 1924

▼

MUSHROOM RAGOUT ON FOUR COLORS

serves six

Butter or margarine	2 tbsp.	30 g
Onions, finely chopped	4 tsp.	20 g
Various mushrooms, whole	2 cups	420 g
White wine	1/4 cup	50 ml
Salt and pepper	to taste	to taste

Melt the butter or margarine, add the chopped onions and then the mushrooms. Toss for two minutes. Deglaze with wine and season to taste.

Sauces

Butter or margarine	2 tsp.	10 g
Onions, chopped	2 tsp.	10 g
Red peppers, chopped	3/4 cup	180 g
White wine	3 tbsp.	40 ml
Chicken stock	2/3 cup	150 ml
Corn starch	1 tsp.	5 g
Whipping cream	3 tbsp.	40 g
(mix corn starch with cream)		
Salt and pepper	to taste	to taste

Sauté the onions and peppers on medium heat for 5 minutes. Deglaze with wine, add the chicken stock and reduce by 1/3. Put in a blender until all color is gone from peppers. Bring back to a boil, add the cream and starch mixture and let simmer for 2 minutes. Strain through a fine sieve and season with salt and pepper.

For the other 3 sauce colors, substitute green, yellow and orange peppers and repeat.

Gerhard Frey, Executive Chef
Mount Royal Hotel, Banff

▲

▼

Lunch at Lake O'Hara, *Vaux Family photograph,* 1897

▲

▼

Soups and Salads

▼

POPPY SEED LEMON YOGURT DRESSING

makes about two cups

Kraft miracle whip dressing	1 cup	250 ml
Plain yogurt	1 cup	250 ml
Grated rind and juice of lemon	1	1
Poppy seeds	1/4 cup	50 ml
Fresh chopped parsley	2 tbsp.	30 ml
Cayenne pepper	pinch	pinch
Oregano leaves, whole leaf rubbed	1 tsp.	5 ml
Liquid honey	1 tbsp.	30 ml

Fresh ground pepper, couple of twists

Mix all ingredients together. Stores well in the refrigerator for weeks. Can be thinned with a little water before use if dressing is too thick.

Jerry Cook
Lake Louise Station Restaurant, Lake Louise

"Miette Sulphur Springs....One case worthy of mention was a man who was unable to walk when he commenced taking the treatment, but who in a couple of weeks was able to cover on foot the 12 miles of trail between the springs and Pocahontas. He stated that he had suffered from rheumatism for a number of years without being able to get any relief, but after a month's stay he was able to return home apparently entirely cured."

R.S. Stronach, acting Superintendent of Jasper Park in his yearly report for 1918-19

▲

Waterton Lake
Waterton Lakes National Park

▼

RASPBERRY AND BALSAMIC VINAIGRETTE

makes about two cups of dressing

Olive oil	1 cup	250 ml
Balsamic vinegar	1/4 cup	50 ml
Raspberry vinegar	1/4 cup	50 ml
Red wine	1/4 cup	50 ml
Honey	3 tbsp.	45 ml
Dijon mustard	1 tbsp.	15 ml
Tabasco sauce	to taste	to taste
Worcestershire sauce	to taste	to taste
Salt and pepper	to taste	to taste
Lemon juice	to taste	to taste

Whisk all ingredients together and serve as a light dressing over fresh greens of choice.

Scott Schroeder, Executive Chef
Lake O'Hara Lodge, Yoho National Park

"Good old days on the trail....When the coffee pot upset... and the sugar and salt got wet and sometimes the beans went sour and the bacon musty and the wind blew smoke in your eyes...how I wish I could live them all over again!"

Tom Wilson, pioneer Canadian Rockies guide, Banff Crag and Canyon, May 1, 1925

▲

▼

TARRAGON SALAD JULIENNE

serves four

Salad

Carrot	2/3 cup	150 ml
Green pepper	2/3 cup	150 ml
Green onion	2/3 cup	150 ml
Hard boiled egg	1	1
Butter leaf lettuce	1 head	1 head

Slice carrots and green pepper in symmetrical shapes. Finely chop green onions and egg. For each salad, layer the lettuce on the bottom, julienne of vegetables on top then add dressing and garnish with green onions and egg.

Dressing

Mayonnaise	1 cup	250 ml
Tarragon	1/3 cup	80 ml
Honey	1/3 cup	80 ml
Water	3 tbsp	45 ml
Salt	to taste	to taste
White pepper	to taste	to taste

Mix mayonnaise, tarragon and honey in a bowl. Add salt and pepper to taste. Add water slowly and stir until well mixed.

Michel Payant, Sous Chef
Chateau Jasper, Jasper

▼

SPICED BUTTERNUT SQUASH SOUP

serves four

Butternut squash, seeded, peeled and chopped	3 lb.	1.5 kg
Olive oil, as needed		
Brown sugar	to taste	to taste
Salt and pepper	to taste	to taste
Cayenne pepper	to taste	to taste
Carrots, peeled, chopped	2	2
Celery stalks, peeled, chopped	2	2
Garlic cloves, peeled, crushed	3	3
Onion, chopped	1	1
White wine	3/4 cup	175 ml
Vegetable stock, approximately	4 cups	1 l
Salt and pepper	to taste	to taste
Whipping cream (optional)	1/2 cup	125 ml

Spread pieces of butternut squash onto baking sheet and brush with olive oil. Sprinkle with brown sugar, salt and pepper and (sparingly) cayenne pepper. Roast in a preheated 400°F (200°C) oven until golden brown (about 20 minutes).

In a soup pot, sauté onions, carrots, celery and garlic in olive oil (brown slightly). Add white wine and cook for 1 minute. Add roasted squash and cover with vegetable stock. Bring to a boil, reduce heat and cook until all ingredients are tender. Purée in blender or food processor and strain. Return to heat, adjust consistency with more vegetable stock (if necessary). Season with salt and pepper to taste and more cayenne pepper (if desired). Add cream (if desired).

Scott Schroeder, Executive Chef
Lake O'Hara Lodge, Yoho National Park

▲

CHILLED FRUIT SOUPS

Melon Soup

serves approximately four

Cantaloupe, totally puréed	2	2
Honeydew, totally puréed	1/2	1/2
White wine	1 cup	250 ml
Triple sec	to taste	to taste
Nutmeg	to taste	to taste
Cinnamon	to taste	to taste

Combine all ingredients and chill.

Berry Soup

serves approximately four

Frozen berries ....2 - 3 lbs..1 - 1.5 kg
(Any combination of blueberries, raspberries, blackberries and cranberries. Cranberries give a good colour).

Red wine	1 cup	250 ml
Yogurt	3/4 cup	175 ml
Sambuca or Pernod	to taste	to taste
Honey	to taste	to taste
Chopped fresh mint	to taste	to taste

Water, if necessary

Cook berries in red wine until soft. Purée and strain. Add yogurt, liqueur, honey and chopped mint. Chill well. Adjust consistency with water (if necessary). When serving, garnish with fresh mint sprig.

▼

Variation: An interesting effect is created if both soups are poured simultane-
ously and slowly into flat serving bowls. If the consistency of the two soups is
the same, it's easier to keep them from mixing together.

Scott Schroeder, Executive Chef
Lake O'Hara Lodge, Yoho National Park

*"The establishment of the Alpine Club of Canada has already done a great deal to
make the National Park attractive to lovers of mountain climbing. This club, which
was organized at Winnipeg in March last year under excellent auspices, held its first
summer camp at the summit of the Yoho Pass from July 9 to July 16. Over 100
members attended, and the proceedings were entirely successful. The situation was ad-
mirably chosen, only twelve miles from the village of Field, and at the same time in
the heart of the mountains. The weather was perfect throughout, and Edouard and
Gottfried Feuz, the Swiss guides in attendance, did their work most satisfactorily.
Eight of the higher mountain peaks were successfully surmounted, Collie, the
President, the Vice-President, Marpole, Michael's Peak, Wapta, Burgess and Field."*

**(Howard Douglas, Superintendent in his "Report of the Rocky
Mountains Park of Canada" for the year 1906)**

▲

▼

EXOTIC GREENS, PROSCIUTTO WITH LEMON GOAT CHEESE DRESSING

serves two

Salad

Roma tomatoes, vine ripened.........2............2
Exotic greens, 2 large servings

(such as arugula, oak leaf, chicory, swiss chard, nicoise, dandelions - sold in some stores already mixed and bagged under names such as California mix or field mix)

Lemon Goat Cheese Dressing

Fresh goat cheese (St. Chevrier).......1/4 cup..50 ml
Lemon juice....................................2 tbsp.....30 ml
Lemon rind, very finely grated ....1 tbsp.....15 ml
Mayonnaise ....1/2 cup..125 ml
Sour cream ....1/3 cup..75 ml
Fresh chives, chopped ....2 tbsp.....30 ml
Garlic clove, minced ....1............1
Light cream 10% ....2 tbsp.....45 ml
Fresh ground black pepper ....1/2 tsp. ..5 ml
Prosciutto, trimmed, lean, julienne ..2 oz. ......55 g

In a bowl, whisk the goat cheese and lemon juice until smooth consistency, whisk in lemon rind, mayonnaise, sour cream, chives and garlic. Continue to whisk while slowly adding the light cream until desired consistency. Season with salt and pepper to taste. Chill until needed. This dressing may thicken when refrigerated, just thin out with some additional cream.

▲

▼

Arrange the salad greens and Roma tomatoes on chilled plates, sprinkle with julienne of prosciutto and drizzle with lemon goat cheese dressing. Serve with slices of crusty French baguette.

Milos J. Moravcik, Executive Chef
Inns of Banff Park, Banff

PARSNIP, HONEY AND LIME SOUP

serves eight

Vegetable oil	2 tbsp.	30 ml
Small onions, diced	2	2
Parsnips	2 lb.	1 kg
Chicken stock	8 cups	2 l
Honey	1/2 cup	125 ml
Lime	1/2 cup	125 ml
Curry powder	1/2 tsp.	2 ml
Salt and pepper	to taste	to taste

Sauté onions on medium heat until soft. Add peeled and chopped parsnips and stock. Simmer until parsnips are soft. Add remaining ingredients and purée in a blender or food processor. Adjust seasoning and serve hot.

Tom Hayes, Executive Chef
Buffalo Mountain Lodge, Banff

"Waterton: 'inside lake', pukto-na-sikimi in Blackfoot, old name for Waterton Lakes which are inside the first range of the Rocky Mountains."

Indian Names for Alberta Communities by Hugh A. Dempsey, 1987

▲

▼

GREEN CHILI CILANTRO VINAIGRETTE

makes about one cup (250 ml)

Cilantro	1/4 cup	50 ml
Garlic clove	1	1
Green ortega chilies	2 tbsp.	30 ml
Cumin	1/2 tsp.	2 ml
Sugar	1 tsp.	5 ml
Salt	dash	dash
Cayenne	dash	dash
Red wine vinegar	2 tbsp.	3 ml
Orange juice	1 tbsp.	15 ml
Vegetable oil	1/4 cup	50 ml

In a food processor or blender, purée the cilantro, garlic, chilies, cumin, sugar, salt and cayenne. Mix in the vinegar and orange. Then with the processor on, very slowly pour in the vegetable oil until mixture is emulsified.

Greg and Neil Ronaasen
Coyote's Deli & Grill, Banff

"Banff: 'holy springs', nato-oh-siskoom in Blackfoot, named for the hot springs; 'waterfall place', minihapa in Stony, and nipika-pakitik in Cree, named for the falls on Cascade Mountain; and: 'in the mountains', tsa-nidzá in Sarcee."

Indian Names for Alberta Communities by Hugh A. Dempsey

▲

▼

BUMPER'S BEEF BARLEY SOUP

makes fifteen cups

Beef soup base	4 oz.	125 g
Water	8 cups	2 l
Barley	1 cup	250 ml
Whole tomatoes, hand crushed	2 cups	500 ml
Crushed tomatoes	1 cup	250 ml
Tomato juice	1/2 cup	125 ml
Onion, diced to 1/2" (1 cm)	1 cup	250 ml
Celery, diced to 1/2" (1 cm)	1 cup	250 ml
Carrots, diced to 1/2" (1 cm)	1 cup	250 ml
Turnip, diced to 1/2" (1 cm)	1 cup	250 ml
Beef, cut in 1" (2 1/2 cm) cubes and pre-cooked	8 oz.	250 g
Thyme	1/4 tsp.	1 ml
Oregano	1/4 tsp.	1 ml
Garlic powder	1/4 tsp.	1 ml
Basil	1/4 tsp.	1 ml
Worcestershire sauce	1 tsp.	5 ml
Bay leaf	1	1

Bring water to a boil in a 4 quart (4 l) pot and add the beef soup base. Warm barley with warm water to remove excess starch. Strain and add to pot. When barley is cooked about half through, add tomatoes, crushed tomatoes and tomato juice. Then add the diced vegetables, simmering on low heat until vegetables are about half cooked. Add beef cubes and spices and continue simmering until vegetables are well cooked. Remove bay leaf and serve immediately.

This soup can also be cooled and reheated.

Bumper's Beef House Restaurant, Banff

▲

▼

SCALLOP SALAD WITH A BALSAMIC VINAIGRETTE

serves four

Romaine lettuce ....1 head

Red pepper 1

Carrot 1

Lemon 1

Parsley sprigs 4

Trim and wash romaine, pat leaves dry with a cloth or use salad spinner. Rip leaves in strips 1" (2,5 cm) wide. Place romaine in 4 salad bowls.

Peel the carrot, wash and seed the red pepper, then julienne (cut into match stick size strips). Cut lemon into wedges. Keep aside the lemon, parsley, carrot and red pepper to garnish.

Scallops 24 24

Olive oil ....4 tbsp.....60 ml

Balsamic vinegar ....8 tbsp.....120 ml

Salt ....to taste...to taste

Fresh ground black pepper ....to taste...to taste

Sweet basil ....to taste...to taste

Preheat a 10" (25 cm) pan on medium heat. Add the olive oil and scallops, then season them with salt, pepper and basil. Cook for 5-6 minutes or until done, when they are just firm to the touch. Overcooking the scallops will make them chewy. Then take the pan off the heat, pour in the balsamic vinegar and mix well. Spoon scallops and vinaigrette over the romaine, top with carrot and red pepper julienne and garnish with lemon and parsley sprigs. Serve immediately.

Daniel Martineau, Chef/Partner
Baker Creek Bistro, Lake Louise

▲

▼

MIXED SALAD WITH TARRAGON VINEGAR

Mixed lettuce
Boston leaf
Endive lettuce
Radicchio
Spinach
Butter leaf

Tarragon dressing

White wine vinegar	1/4 cup	50 ml
Olive oil	2/3 cup	150 ml
Shallots	2/3 oz.	20 g
Garlic	2/3 oz.	20 g
Lemon, fresh	to taste	to taste
Tarragon, fresh	2 oz.	50 g
Dijon mustard	2 tbsp.	30 ml
Salt and pepper	to taste	to taste

Place all ingredients in a bowl and stir well. Repeat again just before serving.

Garnish the salad with tomato wedges, cucumber slices or orange wedges.

Claude Harvey, Chef de Cuisine
Joshua's Restaurant, Banff

"I told my wife that if she bobbed her hair I would leave her." "But she bobbed it; and you're still living with her?" "You bet I am. I'll show her that she can't bluff me."

Banff Crag and Canyon, May 1, 1925

▲

▼

GRIZZLY HOUSE SALAD

Butter lettuce
Radishes, sliced
Celery, diced
Carrots, shredded

House Dressing:

Mayonnaise	1 cup	250 ml
Virgin olive oil	2 oz.	55 g
Honey	4 oz.	125 g
Onion powder	1 tsp.	5 ml
Dill weed	2 tbsp.	30 ml
Paprika	2 tsp.	10 ml
Lea + Perrins	dash	dash
White wine tarragon vinegar	2 oz.	55 g
Parsley flakes	1 tsp.	5 ml
Bay leaf, crushed	1	1
Dry mustard	1 tsp.	5 ml

Mix all ingredients well.

Phil Pappin, Chef
Grizzly House, Banff

"The good old Alberta dining room...will on September 3, close its doors...after that date there will be a number of hungry boarders, who frequently eat an awful lot and seldom very little, looking around for a new grub pile."

Banff Crag and Canyon, August 18, 1917

▲

▼

CREME DE VEAU CHASSEUR

serves 10 @ 200 ml per person

Veal, cooked	3 1/2 oz.	100 g
Regular mushrooms	1/2 cup	100 g
Mushrooms, mixed variety (oyster, chanterelle, etc.) cooked and sliced	1/2 cup	125 g
Tomato, cubed	1/2 cup	125 g
Butter	1 tbsp.	15 ml
White wine	1/2 cup	100 ml
Veal broth	9 cups	2 l
Flour	6 tbsp.	90 ml
Whipping cream	4/5 cup	200 ml
Salt and pepper	to taste	to taste
Lemon juice	1/2 tsp.	2 ml

In a sauce pan sauté veal, mushrooms and tomato for about 2 minutes in butter. Add white wine and reduce a bit. Then add veal broth and bring it to a boil. Mix cream and flour together and pour into the soup. Let it simmer for about 15 to 20 minutes and spice with salt, pepper and lemon juice.

Markus Eisenring, Chef/Owner
Peppermill Restaurant, Canmore

▲

▼

QUESO SOPAS (cheese soup)

serves six to eight

All purpose flour	1 cup	250 g
Butter	4 oz.	115 g
Green peppers, diced	1/4 cup	60 ml
Onions, diced	1/4 cup	60 ml
White pepper	1 tsp.	5 ml
Garlic powder	1 tsp.	5 ml
Brick cheese, grated	9 oz.	250 g
Monterey Jack cheese, grated	9 oz.	250 g
Chicken broth	3 1/2 cup	850 ml

Cheddar cheese, grated
Milk

Heat broth. Combine butter, vegetables and spices in a saucepan over high heat and cook until butter is completely melted and vegetables are done. Add flour to butter-vegetables mixture and whisk rapidly until smooth and all butter is absorbed. Add heated broth and stir rapidly until butter-flour mixture dissolves. Let simmer on medium high heat until thickened. Add grated cheese and stir in until smooth. Thin to desire consistency with milk. To serve, top with grated cheddar cheese and broil in oven until nicely browned.

Magpie & Stump Restaurant and Cantina, Banff

▼

WINTER SQUASH SOUP WITH SCALLOPS

serves six to eight

Butter	3 1/2 oz.	100 g
Onions, chopped	10 oz.	280 g
Squash, chopped (banana and corn)	32 oz.	1 kg
Chicken stock	9 cups	2 l
Dry sherry	2/3 cups	150 ml
Cream	2 1/4 cup	500 ml
Salt and pepper	to taste	to taste
Scallops, sliced	6 – 8	6 – 8

In large pot, melt butter and sauté the onions. Add squash and sauté for 5 minutes.

Add sherry and the chicken stock then purée the mixture and pour back. Stir in the cream and season to taste.

Place the sliced scallops on a soup plate and pour the hot soup on top. Garnish with parsley and serve hot.

The Kitchen Brigade
Rimrock Resort Hotel, Banff

"The village dogs seem to have vetoed the order-in-council forbidding them to run at large."

Banff Crag and Canyon, August 22, 1903

▲

▼

SMOKED GRUYERE CHEESE SALAD

serves four to six

Dressing

Olive oil	6 tbsp.	90 ml
Sherry or apple cider vinegar	3 tbsp.	45 ml
Dijon mustard	2 tsp.	10 ml
Maple syrup	1 tbsp.	15 ml
Garlic clove, crushed	1	1
Nutmeg	1/4 tsp.	1 ml
Curry powder	1/2 tsp.	2 ml
Freshly ground black pepper and salt	to taste	to taste

Salad

Romaine lettuce	1 head	1 head
Green onions, finely chopped	2	2
Celery, finely sliced	3 stalks	3 stalks
Apple, diced with	1/2 cup	125 ml
lemon juice	2 tbsp.	30 ml
Carrot, peel and make strips	1	1
Cucumber	slices	slices
Smoked Gruyere cheese, diced	1/2 cup	125 ml
Sunflower seeds, roasted	1/4 cup	50 ml

▲

Moraine Lake
Banff National Park

▼

Wash lettuce and dry in spinner. Dice apple (leaving the skin on) and soak in lemon juice. Peel carrots, make strips with the peeler.

Toast the sunflower seeds in the oven, stirring occasionally. Remove from oven and cool.

Add dressing to salad and garnish with sunflower seeds.

Kim Purdy
Mt. Assiniboine Lodge Cookbook, Mt. Assiniboine Lodge, Mt. Assiniboine Provincial Park

"A cow is a female quadruped with an alto voice and a countenance in which there is no guile. She collaborates with the pump in the production of a liquid called milk, provides filler for hash, and at last, is skinned by those she has benefited, as mortals commonly are."

Banff Crag and Canyon, June 15, 1928

▲

▼

BELGIAN ENDIVE AND OAK LEAF SALAD WITH PUMPKIN DRESSING

serves six

Belgian endive	4 pieces
Baby oak leaf lettuce	6 heads
Mini pumpkins	6
Edible flowers	6

Dressing

White wine vinegar	3 tbsp.	40 ml
Walnut oil	4 tsp.	20 ml
Sunflower oil	2/3 cup	150 ml
Pumpkin purée, cooked	4 tbsp.	60 g
Water	2 tsp.	10 ml
Sugar	1 tbsp.	15 g
Salt and pepper	to taste	to taste

Put all the ingredients through a blender, then a sieve. Let the dressing rest over night before adding the salt and pepper.

To serve: Use only the top of the Belgian endive (cut in half length wise) and mix with the washed baby oak leaf lettuce.

Cut off the top of the pumpkins and hollow out. Toss the salad in the dressing and arrange in pumpkins and place lids back on, covering 1/3 of the pumpkin. Garnish with the flower or flower petals.

Note: A very nice addition to the salad is thinly sliced smoked duck breast or poached shrimp.

Gerhard Frey, Executive Chef
Mount Royal Hotel, Banff

▲

▼

RASPBERRY VINAIGRETTE

Salad oil	3 cups	700 ml
Raspberry vinegar	1 cup	200 ml
Onion, finely chopped	1	1
Garlic clove, finely chopped	1	1
Mustard	1 tsp	5 ml
Honey	2 tsp	10 ml
Salt and Pepper	to taste	to taste

Mix all ingredients well.

Jean-Luc Schwendener, Chef
Mount Engadine Lodge, Kananaskis Country

"*Man is a social animal, he loves to get in bunches of his own kind, and when…people see that big crowds are coming to Banff, they say to themselves 'the people are going to Banff…', and away they go.*

Banff Crag and Canyon, September, 1917

▼

GRILLED BELGIAN ENDIVE SALAD WITH SEA SCALLOPS AND ROASTED TOMATO AND GARLIC DRESSING

four servings

Dressing

Roma tomatoes	2	2
Head of garlic	1	1
Balsamic vinegar	1/4 cup	50 ml
Virgin olive oil	1/4 cup	50 ml
Chicken stock	1/4 cup	50 ml
Salt	pinch	pinch
Fresh ground pepper	to taste	to taste

Cut the top of the garlic head to expose the flesh. Wrap the garlic, without peeling, in tinfoil and bake in the oven or on the BBQ until tender. When done, squeeze the garlic out of the shell and reserve.

Cut the tomatoes lengthwise in half and roast with a little olive oil in the oven or on the BBQ. When done remove the skin and seeds and place together with the garlic in a blender. Add the balsamic vinegar, salt, pepper and slowly add the olive oil while the blender is running.

Scallops

Large scallops	16 - 20	16 - 20
Lemon, juice	1/2	1/2
Virgin olive oil	4 tsp.	20 ml
Salt	pinch	pinch
Fresh ground pepper	to taste	to taste

Put the scallops on 4 skewers and marinate with above listed ingredients for 30 minutes.

▲

▼

Belgian endive

Heads of Belgian endive, quartered lengthwise	4	4
Olive oil	2 tbsp.	30 ml
Salt	pinch	pinch
Fresh ground pepper	to taste	to taste

Butter lettuce hearts

Oak leaf lettuce

Drizzle olive oil over the quartered Belgian endive and season with salt and pepper.

Preparation: On moderate heat, grill or BBQ the Belgian endive and the scallops for 3 to 4 minutes on 2 sides. Do not overcook. The endive should be crunchy.

On each of the 4 dinner plates lay out 3 to 4 butter lettuce hearts and oak leaf lettuce as a base. Place 4 of the warm Belgian endive on each of the plates and divide the scallops on top by pushing them off the skewers.

To finish the plates, drizzle the warm dressing over the salad and sprinkle with chopped chives.

Martin Luthi, Executive Chef
Banff Springs Hotel, Banff

"The initial moonlight trip to Lake Minnewanka ... 60 ladies and gentlemen started out from the King Edward Hotel ... in Tally-hos, democrats, and buggies, a small orchestra also going out ... (to) the old chalet for supper ... after which dancing kept up till it was time for the return journey, home being safely reached shortly after two a.m."

Banff Crag and Canyon, June 25, 1912

▲

▼

CARROT GINGER SOUP WITH MUSSELS AND SCALLOPS

serves six

Garlic clove, crushed	1	1
Red onion, medium, diced	1/2	1/2
Young carrots, peeled and diced	14 oz.	400 g
Ginger, fresh, peeled and sliced	2/3 oz.	20 g
Olive oil	2 tbsp.	25 ml
Mussels, in shell cleaned, washed	12	12
Scallops, large or medium	12	12
Dry white wine	1/2 cup	100 ml
Chicken stock	5 cups	1,2 l
Cream	1/2 cup	100 ml
Salt and pepper	to taste	to taste
Plain yogurt	6 tbsp.	90 ml
Cilantro, chopped	2 tsp.	10 ml

In a sauce pan heat up 2 tbsp. (25 ml) olive oil on medium heat. Add the carrots, onions, garlic and sauté to a golden color. Add the ginger, scallops, mussels and sauté for 1 more minute.

Add the white wine and reduce until almost dry. Then add the chicken stock and bring to a boil. When the mussels open, remove with the scallops and reserve. Simmer the rest until the vegetables are tender. Then place it into a blender, add the cream and blend until the soup is smooth. Pour the soup back into the pan, reheat and season with salt and pepper.

Divide the mussels and scallops equally into 6 soup plates and pour the hot soup over the seafood. Put a tablespoon of yogurt into the center of each plate and sprinkle with cilantro.

Martin Luthi, Executive Chef
Banff Springs Hotel, Banff

▲

▼

NORTHERN MUSHROOM SOUP

serves four

Button mushrooms	2 lb.	900 g
Medium onion, finely diced	1	1
Garlic cloves, finely chopped	2	2
Butter	1/2 cup	125 ml
All purpose flour	1/2 cup	125 ml
Dry white wine	1 cup	250 ml
Chicken stock	1 qt.	1000 ml
Whipping cream	1 cup	250 ml
Honey	1 tsp.	5 ml
Rosemary, fresh sprigs	2	2
Salt and pepper	to taste	to taste

Prepare the mushrooms for cooking: Wash and slice the button mushrooms, place on a towel and let dry before cooking.

In a heavy bottomed sauce pan melt the butter, add the diced onion, garlic and cook until lightly browned. Add the flour and incorporate completely and smoothly into the butter. Cook the roux for 2 to 3 minutes stirring constantly so it does not burn. Add your chicken stock and incorporate the stock into the roux, being careful not to leave any lumps, the consistency should be smooth.

In a separate heavy bottomed pot, melt some butter and sauté the mushrooms over medium to high heat. Once the mushrooms have cooked, add the wine to help remove all the goodness from the bottom of the pan. Once the wine has reduced by half add all the mushrooms, honey, whipping cream and rosemary to the soup.

Season with salt and pepper. Simmer for 30 minutes on low heat. The soup is then ready to serve.

David MacGillivray, Executive Chef
Jasper Park Lodge, Jasper

▼

BUTTERMILK BAKING POWDER BISCUITS TO SERVE WITH NORTHERN MUSHROOM SOUP

makes 1 dozen

All purpose flour	.2 cups	....500 ml
Baking powder	.2 tsp.	.......10 ml
Baking soda	.1/4 tsp.	..1 ml
Salt	.1/4 tsp.	..1 ml
Stick margarine, chilled		
cut into small pieces	.3 1/2 tbsp.	50 ml
Low-fat buttermilk	.3/4 cup	..175 ml

Combine flour and next 3 ingredients in a bowl, cut in chilled margarine with a pastry blender until the mixture resembles coarse meal. Add buttermilk, and stir just until dry ingredients are moistened.

Turn dough out onto a floured surface, knead 4 or 5 times. Roll dough to 1/2" (12 mm) thickness; cut with a 2 1/2"

(6 cm) biscuit cutter. Place on baking sheet and bake at 450°F (230°C) for 12 minutes or until golden brown.

If you like, you can add chopped fresh herbs such a basil, thyme or rosemary to the dough to give it a unique flavor.

David MacGillivray, Executive Chef
Jasper Park Lodge, Jasper National Park

"It should be understood that the mattresses on the Bankhead rifle range were placed there for the use of the club members when shooting, and for no other purpose.:

Banff Crag and Canyon, August 11, 1906

▼

SALAD EAGLES NEST

Ingredients for Dressing

Olive oil...3 parts

Balsamic vinegar ....1 part

Dijon mustard ....to taste

Peppercorns, cracked ....to taste

Basil ....to taste

Capers, chopped.............................to taste

Garlic ....to taste

Salt ....to taste

Mix oil and vinegar in mixing bowl, add enough Dijon mustard to emulsify the dressing. Add to taste the remaining ingredients.

Ingredients for Salad

Radicchio lettuce

Butter lettuce

Pine nuts

Diced red pepper

Pink grapefruit sections

Toss radicchio and butter lettuce in dressing and arrange on plates. Fan out grapefruit sections decoratively along edge of plate, sprinkle pine nuts and red pepper on top of salad and serve.

Michael Clark, Executive Chef
Sunshine Village, Banff National Park

▼

COLD CORN SOUP WITH SMOKED SALMON

serves ten

Butter	3 1/2 oz.	100 g
Onions, sliced	3 1/2 oz.	100 g
Sweet corn kernels	28 oz.	800 g
White wine	4/5 cup	200 ml
Bourbon whiskey	1/2 cup	100 ml
Vegetable or chicken stock	4 1/3 cup	1 l
Whipping cream	1 3/4 cup	400 ml
Sugar	1/3 cup	75 ml
Salt and white pepper	to taste	to taste
Puff pastry	7 oz.	200 g
Egg yolks	2	2
Smoked salmon	7 oz.	200 g
Russian caviar	1 jar	1 jar
Fresh dill	1 bunch	1 bunch

Melt butter in a skillet and sauté onions and corn. Stir in wine and whiskey, then add stock, cream and sugar. Season with salt, pepper and fresh dill, cook for 20 minutes. After cooling, blend and strain through fine sieve.

While soup is cooling, roll out the puff pastry on some flour and cut out little figures (e.g. fish shapes) egg wash and bake at 380°F (190°C) for 3 to 4 minutes until lightly brown. After cooling, cut them in half and fill with a little caviar (like a mini sandwich). Before serving, garnish soup plate rim with smoked salmon and fresh dill, place puff pastry figures in the middle of the soup.

Mario Thom, Chef
Le Beaujolais, Banff

▼

OKONOKI SALAD

Romaine lettuce	1 head
Tomatoes, diced	2
Avocado, diced	2

Clean and cut lettuce leaves into bite size pieces. Toss in tomato, avocado and Saskatoon Vinaigrette Dressing.

SASKATOON VINAIGRETTE DRESSING

Saskatoon berries	1/2 cup	125 ml
Red wine	4 tbsp.	60 ml
Garlic	1 tbsp.	15 ml
Vinegar	4 tbsp.	60 ml
Olive oil	4 tbsp.	60 ml
Basil paste	1 tbsp.	15 ml
Sugar	2 tbsp.	30 ml
Parsley	1 tbsp.	15 ml
Salt and pepper	to taste	to taste

Combine all ingredients and purée in blender.

Robert Frost, Executive Chef
Kilmorey Lodge, Waterton

"The only work done in the Waterton Park was the cutting of a good horse trail, six feet wide and six miles long, from Cameron Falls in the park to the International boundary line. Tourists can now ride through to the road in Glacier Park and the boundary line can be patrolled so as to prevent poaching from the American side."

Howard Douglas, Commissioner of Dominion Parks in his "Commissioner of Dominion Parks, 1911.

Dining at the Banff Springs, *Brigden photograph,* 1924

Entrées

▼

FRESH SALMON SPIRAL WITH SUNDRIED TOMATO HERB BUTTER

serves six

Sundried Tomato Herb Butter

Sundried tomatoes	2 tbsp.	30 ml
Hot water	1 cup	250 ml
Fresh thyme	1 tsp.	5 ml
Fresh basil leaves	5 - 6	5 - 6
Fresh rosemary	a few sprigs	
Garlic clove	1	1
Salt and pepper	to taste	to taste
Butter	1/4 lb	110 g

Soak sundried tomatoes in hot water until soft then drain. Process tomatoes, all herbs, garlic and butter in food processor to smooth consistency. Salt and pepper to taste then transfer to small piping bag with star tip.

Salmon

Fresh salmon, boned & skinned........1 side .....1 side

Olive oil, as needed

White wine, enough to cover bottom of baking dish

Preheat oven to 400°F. Cut side of salmon lengthwise into 1/2" to 3/4" (1.2 to 1.6 cm) strips and arrange in coils. Transfer to oven proof baking tray. (A side usually yields 6 to 7 servings.) Brush salmon coils with olive oil. Season with salt and pepper. Cover bottom of baking dish with white wine then cover baking dish tightly with foil wrap. Bake 20 to 30 minutes. Transfer salmon to serving plates. Pipe butter onto hot salmon and serve immediately. Serve with rice and seasonal vegetables.

Option: Omit piping bag and refrigerate butter to be cut into serving sizes at time of service.

Scott Schroeder, Executive Chef
Lake O'Hara Lodge, Yoho National Park

▲

BASIL SAUCE - PESTO

about eight servings

Grated parmesan cheese..................3/4 cup ..175 ml

Grated pecorino romano cheese.......1/4 cup ..50 ml

Fresh basil leaves, lightly packed.......3 cups ....750 ml

Pine nuts or chopped walnuts ....1/2 cup ..125 ml

Garlic cloves...................................3 - 4.......3 - 4

Sea salt ....1/2 tsp. ..2 ml

Freshly ground black pepper,...........to taste

Extra virgin olive oil ....1 cup .....250 ml

Grind the cheeses, basil, nuts, garlic, salt and pepper together in a food processor. Gradually add the olive oil until a thick sauce is obtained. Serve with your favourite pasta.

The sauce will keep if put in a sealed jar and stored in a cool place.

Variation: Add 2 tbsp. of lemon juice or vinegar and 3 tbsp. of oil and use as a salad dressing for cold pasta salad.

Mike Derondeau, Owner
Guido's Ristorante, Banff

"But, as fate would have it, someone had dropped a pat of butter on one of the two steps which lead into the room and, as happens once in every waiter's life...(Oscar) and the fish went down together. To the not-so-dulcet sound of some not-so-polite snickers. Oscar pieced the fish together and proceeded to Reynold's table where he served the meal as best as he could with one arm — the other had been broken in the fall!"

An episode in the life of the extraordinarily dedicated 1920's waiter Oscar, by Bart Robinson, in his *Banff Springs — The Story of a Hotel*; Summerthought, Ltd., Banff, 1973

▼

BAKED CHICKEN BREAST WITH FRESH BASIL AND ROASTED GARLIC

serves six

Garlic cloves	6 - 7	6 - 7
Olive oil, as needed		
Chicken breasts, boneless, skinless	6	6
White wine	3/4 cup	175 ml
Fresh basil, coarse chopped	2 tbsp.	30 ml
Salt and pepper	to taste	to taste
Butter	2 tbsp.	30 ml

Peel and crush garlic cloves (remove tough stems and sprouts). Place crushed cloves in a small oven proof dish, sprinkle with salt, cover with olive oil and bake until garlic softens and begins to brown. Strain garlic out of olive oil, save the oil. Crush garlic into paste with fork.

In a skillet brown chicken breasts in saved garlic olive oil, then transfer chicken to oven proof baking dish. Deglaze the skillet with white wine and cook for 1 minute. Remove from heat, add roasted garlic and chopped basil. Stir in butter. Pour over chicken and season with salt and pepper. Cover baking dish with foil wrap and bake for 15 to 20 minutes in a preheated 400°F(200°C) oven.

Transfer to serving plates with a little of the baking juices and garnish with more fresh basil.

Can be served with Swiss Potatoes (recipe on next page).

Scott Schroeder, Executive Chef
Lake O'Hara Lodge, Yoho National Park

▲

Maligne Lake
Jasper National Park

SWISS POTATOES

serves six
Butter, to coat baking dish
Milk ....1 cup .....250 ml
Whipping cream............................3/4 cup ..200 ml
Garlic cloves, peeled, crushed ....2.............2
Salt and pepper ....to taste...to taste
Nutmeg.......................................to taste...to taste
Cayenne pepper............................to taste...to taste
Starchy potatoes
(small, red skinned potatoes) ....about 8 ..about 8

Butter a 9" x 13" (22 x 33 cm) baking dish.

Place milk, cream, garlic and spices in a medium sauce pan. Peel and slice potatoes into milk mixture and heat on stove top to boiling (milk and cream will begin to thicken with potato starch).

Pour into baking dish making sure all potatoes are submerged. Place on bottom rack of a 325°F(170°C) preheated oven. Bake 1 1/2 hours until consistency is thick and creamy and top is lightly browned.

Scott Schroeder, Executive Chef
Lake O'Hara Lodge, Yoho National Park

"Scientists predict that in 100 years there will be nothing in the world to laugh at. But they're wrong because 100 years from now the people will laugh every time they think of us."
Banff Crag and Canyon, March 7, 1923

▼

VEGETABLE KORMA

serves six

Lentils (red or green)	2/3 cup	150 ml
Vegetable oil	2 tbsp.	30 ml
Garlic cloves, finely diced	2	2
Onion, cubed	1 cup	250 ml
Apple, peeled & finely diced	1 cup	250 ml
Indian curry paste or powder	3 tbsp.	45 ml
Fresh ginger, finely chopped	1 tsp.	5 ml
Cardamom seeds	1 tsp.	5 ml

Assorted fresh vegetables, cubed	4 cups	1 l

(use your choice of vegetables currently available, such as cauliflower, carrots, celery, yams, turnips, potatoes, beans, asparagus, zucchini, mushrooms)

Unsweetened pineapple juice	2 cups	500 ml
Coconut milk	13 oz.	398 ml
Tomato paste	1 tbsp.	15 ml
Mango chutney (any variety)	2 tbsp.	30 ml
Fresh lemon or lime juice	3 tbsp.	45 ml
Light soya sauce	1/2 cup	125 ml

Fresh or dried chilies	to taste	to taste
Salt	to taste	to taste
Corn or potato starch	1 tbsp.	15 ml
White wine or sherry	1/4 cup	50 ml

▲

In a small pot of rapidly boiling salted water, cook the lentils until tender. Drain and set aside. In a large pot, heat the oil, and fry the garlic, onions and apples until translucent. Add the curry, ginger and cardamom, cook briefly, stirring to prevent the mixture from burning on the bottom of the pot.

Add the liquid ingredients and bring to a gentle boil. For hotter tastes, you may now add the chilies - the more you add, the hotter the Korma! Add the root vegetables from your selection and simmer until they are cooked "al dente". Then add the soft vegetables and greens from your selection, and the cooked lentils, and simmer for 10 more minutes. It is important not to add all the vegetables at the same time, to avoid overcooking and discolouration of the more delicate vegetables! Adjust the seasoning by adding salt or more soya sauce, and thicken, if desired with the starch mixed into the wine.

Serve accompanied with Patna or Basmati Rice, Raita (recipe follows) and Nan or Pita Bread.

RAITA

makes 3 cups

Plain yogurt	2 cup	500 ml
Cucumber, peeled and shredded	1 cup	250 ml
Garlic clove, finely chopped	1	1
Onion, finely diced	1 tbsp.	30 ml
Fresh mint, chopped	1 tsp.	5 ml
Salt	to taste	to taste

Choose a good quality yogurt, preferably a "natural" variety. Remove and discard the whey (the watery liquid that has separated from the curd). Place the shredded cucumber in a fine sieve, and allow the juice to drain. You may add the juice to your Korma, if desired. Combine the drained cucumber, yogurt and other ingredients. Keep well chilled until time to serve.

Chris Montgomery
The Sherwood House, Canmore

▼

CHICKEN BREAST WITH GOAT CHEESE AND SUNDRIED TOMATO SALSA

serves four

Chicken breasts, skinless, boneless (6 oz. each)	4	4
Fresh goat cheese (St. Chevrier)	5 oz	140 g
Quark cheese	2 oz	55 g
Garlic cloves, minced	3	3
Chives, finely chopped	2 tbsp.	30 ml
Freshly ground black pepper	1/2 tsp.	2 ml
Olive oil	3 tbsp.	45 ml
Salt	1 tsp.	5 ml

Place chicken breasts skin side down on your work table, with a tenderizer gently pound them out until they increase in size by 1/3. In a bowl mix together the goat cheese, quark, garlic and chives. Divide the cheese mixture among the 4 breasts and spread the cheese in the centre of each breast, leaving 1/2" border from the edge. Fold each breast over to seal in the cheese mixture and season with salt and pepper.

Heat the olive oil in a heavy skillet over medium heat, place the chicken in the heated oil and cook until golden brown, approximately 5 to 6 minutes on each side. Remove from pan and serve with a generous amount of sundried tomato salsa (recipe follows).

▲

SUNDRIED TOMATO SALSA

makes approximately three cups

Sundried tomatoes, diced	1/2 cup	125 ml
Red onion, diced	1/4 cup	50 ml
Jalapeño pepper, seeded & diced	1	1
Cilantro, chopped	1/4 cup	50 ml
Fresh lime juice	1 tsp.	5 ml
Rice wine vinegar	1/4 cup	50 ml
Tomatoes, diced	1 1/2 cup	375 ml
Garlic clove, minced	1	1
Sugar	1 tsp.	2 ml
Coarse salt	1/2 tsp.	2 ml
Freshly ground black pepper	1/8 tsp.	1/2 ml

Mix all ingredients in a bowl. Allow salsa to set for 2 to 3 hours. Serve at room temperature.

Milos J. Moravcik, Executive Chef
Inns of Banff Park, Banff

"The writer who wrote...that the Canadian Rockies have the grandeur and beauty of the Alps, but lack the romance and poetry, has a long guess coming...Regarding romance and poetry, it largely depends on the number of summer girls around."

Banff Crag and Canyon, August 2, 1912

▼

SALMON STUFFED CHICKEN BREAST

serves four

Chicken breasts, boneless, skinless	4	4

Salmon

Sesame seed oil	1 tsp.	5 ml
Olive oil	2 tbsp.	30 ml
Garlic, fresh, finely chopped	1 tsp.	5 ml
Crushed chilies	1/2 tsp.	2 ml
Salmon fillet, boneless	1	1
Fresh chopped parsley	2 tbsp.	30 ml
Fresh ground black pepper	1 tsp.	5 ml

Breading

Flour	1 cup	250 ml
Thyme	pinch	pinch
Salt	1/2 tsp.	5 ml
Fresh ground black pepper	1/2 tsp.	5 ml
Eggs	2 to 3	2 to 3
Milk or cream	1 tbsp.	30 ml
White unsliced bread	1 loaf	1 loaf
Olive oil, for deep frying	6 cups	1.5 l

The night before: Put the loaf of bread in the freezer to make it easier to handle. Mix the sesame seed oil, olive oil, garlic and chilies. Pour over the salmon. Marinate the salmon overnight in the refrigerator.

▲

Make an incision about the width of two fingers into the thickest part of the chicken breast. (Put knife in and fan across and then pull out.)

Cut the salmon fillet into four finger size portions. Mix the parsley and pepper in a bowl. Roll the chunks of salmon in this to coat. Stuff salmon inside the incision in the chicken.

Mix the flour, thyme, salt and pepper together. In a separate bowl whip the eggs and milk or cream.

Take the bread out of the freezer and cut off the crust. Then cut the loaf into 3 pieces. Put through a hand grater, food processor or blender.

Coat the stuffed chicken with the seasoned flour and then the egg mixture and finally lightly pat in bread crumbs. Shake off excess. Heat olive oil in a wok or deep fryer to 400°F(200°C). There should be a light smoke coming off the oil. Put each piece of chicken in for 1 to 2 minutes until golden brown. Put on tray with paper towel to collect excess olive oil. Chicken can be refrigerated overnight or up to 2 to 3 days.

Bake in a preheated 350°F(180°C) oven for 10 to 15 minutes before serving.

Jerry Cook
Lake Louise Station Restaurant, Lake Louise

"It should be understood that the mattresses on the Bankhead rifle range were placed there for the use of the club members when shooting, and for no other purpose.

Banff Crag and Canyon, August 11, 1906

▼

FETTUCCINE WITH TOMATO BASIL CREAM

serves two

Whipping cream	1/2 cup	125 ml
Chicken broth	1/2 cup	125 ml
Water	1/3 cup	75 ml
Olive oil	1/4 cup	50 ml
Tomatoes, seeded & chopped	1 1/2 cup	375 ml
Fresh basil leaves, julienne strips	1/3 cup	75 ml
Dried fettuccine	8 oz	250 g
Freshly grated pecorino romano cheese	2 tbsp.	30 ml
Freshly ground black pepper	1 tsp.	5 ml

In an large pan combine the cream, the broth, water and the oil, bring the liquid to a boil, and cook the mixture at a high simmer for 6 to 7 minutes. Add the basil and tomatoes and simmer the mixture for 1 to 2 minutes.

Cook fettuccine in a big pot of boiling salted water until "al dente" and drain well.

Place fettuccine in the pan with the sauce. Add the romano cheese and coat it well.

Milos J. Moravcik, Executive Chef
Inns of Banff Park, Banff

▲

APPLE MARINATED CORNISH GAME HENS

serves four

Apple juice	4 cups	1 l
Cider vinegar	1 cup	250 ml
Calvados (an apple brandy from France)	3/4 cup	175 ml
Cornish game hens	4	4
Whipping cream	1 cup	250 ml
Apples	2	2
Butter	2 tbsp.	30 ml
Salt and pepper	to taste	to taste

Mix apple juice, vinegar and Calvados. Split game hens down the back and remove back bone and wing tips. Spread open and flatten. Marinate hens for 24 hours, turning occasionally.

Place hens skin side up on a baking sheet and roast in a preheated 375°F(190°C) oven until done, about 30 to 35 minutes. Meanwhile, reduce 1 cup of the marinade with the cream to half of its volume. Slice apples and sauté in butter. Serve hens on top of apple and pour cream sauce over top. Serve with rice, barley or potato and vegetable.

Tom Hayes, Executive Chef
Buffalo Mountain Lodge, Banff

"The student of human nature will find many subjects of interest on the trails in and out of Banff."

Banff Crag and Canyon, July 14, 1912

▲

▼

HEARTY MOUSSAKA

serves twenty-four to twenty-eight

Potatoes	10	10
Eggplant	5	5
Zucchini	6	6
Oil, as needed		
Salt and pepper	to taste	to taste
Meat sauce, recipe follows		
Cream sauce, recipe follows		

Peel and slice potatoes lengthwise. Slice eggplant lengthwise. Cut zucchini in long strips. Sauté vegetables separately in oil until lightly browned. Place on paper toweling in layers to drain well. Cover bottom of 12" x 16 1/2" (30 x 42 cm) baking dish with layer of half the potatoes, season with salt and pepper, add layer of half the eggplant and layer of half the zucchini, seasoning each layer with salt and pepper. Pour meat sauce over top, spread to completely cover zucchini. Repeat layers and seasoning, using all the vegetables. Pour cream sauce over top, spread to completely cover zucchini.

Bake in a preheated 400°F(200°C) oven until vegetables are tender and sauce is golden brown.

Variations: Eggplant may be omitted if desired or moussaka can be made using only eggplant.

Meat Sauce

Ground meat	1 1/2 lb	750 g
Oil	3 tbsp.	45 ml
Onions, chopped	2 - 3	2 - 3
Garlic cloves, minced	3 - 4	3 - 4
Salt and pepper	to taste	to taste
Tomato juice	2 cups	500 ml

▲

▼

Sauté ground meat in oil in frying pan. Add onions, garlic, salt and pepper, simmer for 10 to 15 minutes. Stir in tomato juice, simmer for at least 30 minutes.

Cream Sauce

Milk	4 cups	1 l
Flour	3/4 cup	750 ml
Salt	1 tsp.	5 ml
Butter	1/4 cup	50 ml
Egg yolks	4	4

Pour milk in saucepan, stir in flour until dissolved. Place over medium heat, cook, stirring constantly until mixture comes to a boil and thickens, stir in salt. Remove from heat. Add butter, stir well until melted. Add egg yolks, one at a time, stirring well after each addition.

Tom and Maria Lambropoulos, Owners
Balkan, The Greek Restaurant, Banff

"Canmore: 'shooting at a young spruce tree', too-wup-chinchin- koodibee in Stony; when the Indians were camped on Canmore flats, young boys practiced by shooting at a young tree."

Indian Names for Alberta Communities by Hugh A. Dempsey, 1987

▲

▼

CARIBOU LOIN WITH PEPPERCORN CRUST
SERVED WITH RED CURRANT, CALVADOS GLAZE

serves two

Caribou loin	8 oz	250 g
Whole black peppercorns, crushed	1 oz	30 g
Dijon mustard	2 tbsp.	30 ml
Red currants	2 tbsp.	30 ml
Calvados	2 tbsp.	30 ml
Game stock	3/4 cup	175 ml
Olive oil	2 tbsp.	30 ml
Salt and pepper	to taste	to taste
Red wine	2 tbsp.	30 ml

Season caribou with salt and pepper, brush with Dijon mustard and sprinkle with the crushed whole peppercorns. In a medium saucepan place olive oil and heat until very hot. Sear the caribou in the hot oil. Remove from pan and place in a 350°F(180°C) preheated oven. Cook to preference. Pour excess oil from the pan and deglaze with red wine. Add Calvados and flambé. Add game stock and reduce until sauce is thickened. Add red currants, season to taste and pour over caribou loin.

Aaron Cundliffe, Executive Chef
Emerald Lake Lodge, Yoho National Park

"Some hungry mortal made a raid on a cargo of beef...last night. Whoever was the culprit, he showed his epicurean propensities by leisurely cutting out the choicest bits."

Banff Crag and Canyon, December 29, 1901

▲

▼

STUFFED SALMON

serves 6

Stuffing

Melted butter	1/4 cup	50 ml
Onion, finely chopped	1	1
Celery stalks, finely chopped	2	2
Garlic cloves, minced	2	2
Mushrooms, finely chopped	2 cups	500 ml
Dill	1 tbsp.	15 ml
Toasted almonds	1/2 cup	250 ml
Cooked rice	2 cups	500 ml
Parmesan cheese	1/2 cup	125 ml
Sour cream	1/2 cup	125 ml
Fresh parsley, finely chopped	1 tbsp.	15 ml

Mix stuffing ingredients. Set aside.

Herb butter

Soya sauce	2 tbsp.	30 ml
Garlic cloves, minced	2	2
Dill	1 tbsp.	15 ml
Melted butter	1/2 cup	250 ml

Heat all ingredients of herb butter and set aside.

Fillets of 12"-14"(30-35 cm) salmon ...6 6

Fresh lemon juice

Place the stuffing on an oval oven-proof platter and brush with 1/3 of the herb butter. Drape the salmon fillets over the stuffing. Brush fillets with fresh lemon juice and cover with foil. Bake in a preheated oven at 400°F(200°C) for 50 to 60 minutes, brush with remaining herb butter and garnish with lemon slices and parsley.

Skoki Lodge, Banff National Park

▲

▼

CANADIAN MOUNTAIN STEW

serves 6 to 8

Stewing beef, cubed	3 lb	1 1/2 kg
Water	8 cups	2 l
Beef gravy base	4 oz	125 g
Flour	3 oz	85 g
Carrots, cubed	1 1/2 cup	375 ml
Celery, cubed	1 1/2 cup	375 ml
Onion, cubed	1 1/2 cup	375 ml
Turnip, cubed	1 1/2 cup	375 ml
Potato, cubed	1 1/2 cup	375 ml
Whole mushrooms, canned or fresh	1 cup	250 ml
Red wine	1/2 cup	125 ml
Paprika	1/4 tsp.	1 ml
Oregano	1/4 tsp.	1 ml
Black pepper	1/4 tsp.	1 ml
Basil	1/4 tsp.	1 ml
Thyme	1/4 tsp.	1 ml
Bay leaf	1	1

In a large pot over a high heat, brown meat until cooked completely through. Reduce heat to medium. Stir in flour and allow to cook into beef cubes.

In another pot, add beef base to water and bring to boil. Add to meat and stir until flour is well mixed in.

Skim off any fat or flour lumps from surface.

▲

▼

Add the vegetables, except for the potatoes, and cook on a medium heat until about half done. Add the potatoes and spices and simmer until vegetables are cooked through.

Then add the red wine and mushrooms. Simmer for about 5 minutes, If further thickening is desired, stir in a mixture of 2 tbsp. (30 ml) flour and 2 tbsp. (30 ml) red wine.

Remove bay leaf and serve immediately.

Bumper's Beef House Restaurant, Banff

"Crowds thronged the sidewalks and parking spaces for autos were difficult to find at times."

Banff Crag and Canyon, May 25, 1928

▲

▼

CURRY GLAZED PORK CHOPS
serves six to eight

Pork chops, trimmed	8	8
Large onion, chopped	1/2	1/2
Cornstarch	1 1/2tbsp.	20 ml
Brown sugar	2 tbsp.	30 ml
Curry powder	1 tbsp.	15 ml
Cinnamon	1 tbsp.	15 ml
Salt	1 tsp.	5 ml
Beef bouillon cube	1	1
Water	1 cup	250 ml
Ketchup	2 tbsp.	30 ml
Strained apricots, (purée of drained canned apricots)	4 oz	115 g

Brown chops in a hot pan and season with salt and pepper to taste. Remove and lay in casserole dish.

Add a little oil to the pan and sauté the onions until translucent. Mix cornstarch, sugar, curry powder, cinnamon and salt together and then stir into pan mixture.

Add water and cook until bubbling. Add bouillon cube and stir until dissolved. Stir in ketchup and apricots.

Pour over chops, cover and bake at 350°F(180°C) for about 45 to 50 minutes.

Serve with steamed cauliflower flowerettes with a light cheese sauce or garnished with buttered bread crumbs.

Lynne Grillmair, Chef
Bugaboo Lodge, Canadian Mountain Holidays

▲

Lake Louise
Banff National Park

▼

BROILED CHICKEN BREAST WITH A STRAWBERRY CANTALOUPE SALSA

serves four

Strawberry Cantaloupe Salsa

Sliced strawberries	2 cups	450 ml
Diced cantaloupe, 1/4" (5 mm)	1 cup	225 ml
Jalapeño, seeded and finely diced	1 or 2	1 or 2
Cilantro sprigs, chopped	5 or 6	5 or 6
Salt	to taste	to taste
Fresh ground black pepper	to taste	to taste
Tabasco	1-2 drops	1-2 drops
Worcestershire	1-2 drops	1-2 drops
Cayenne, small pinch		
Limes, juiced	2	2

Mix ingredients in a bowl and let stand refrigerated for one hour.

Broiled Chicken Breast

Boneless chicken breast, trimmed	4	4
Olive oil	2 tbsp.	30 ml
Lemon juice	2 tbsp.	30 ml
Salt	to taste	to taste
Fresh ground pepper	to taste	to taste
Oregano, small pinch		
Basil, small pinch		
Thyme, small pinch		

Mix all of the above (except the salsa) in a bowl and let sit for a few minutes. Preheat barbecue and cook chicken breasts 6 to 8 minutes on each side. Top chicken with salsa and serve with Mexican fixings (rice, beans, tortilla etc.)

Daniel Martineau, Chef/Partner
Baker Creek Bistro, Lake Louise

▼

HUNTER FONDUE

per serving

Buffalo	3 oz.	85 g
Rabbit	3 oz.	85 g
Venison	3 oz.	85 g

Heat oil in large, heavy fondue pot until hot but not boiling. Dice meat into 1" (2.5 cm) cubes and place on platter. With fondue fork, dip meat into the hot oil and cook to desire.

Serve with the following sauces.

Onion Sauce

Mayonnaise	2 cups	500 ml
White onion, puréed	1/2	1/2
Red onion, puréed	1/2	1/2
Bacon bits	2 oz.	55 g
Chives, 1/2 bunch		
White pepper	pinch	pinch
Onion powder	1 tbsp.	15 ml
Garlic powder	pinch	pinch
Lea + Perrins	1 tsp.	5 ml

Mustard Horseradish

Horseradish	1/2 cup	125 ml
Dijon mustard, strong	1/2 cup	125 ml
Mayonnaise	1 cup	250 ml

Bourguignonne (hot) Sauce

Mayonnaise	3/4 cup	175 ml
Chili sauce	3/4 cup	175 ml

▲

Cayenne	1 tsp	5 ml
Tabasco	1 tsp	5 ml
Dill weed	1 tsp	5 ml
Lea + Perrins	1 tsp	5 ml
Brandy	1 tbsp	15 g

Honey Garlic

Mayonnaise	1 1/2cups	375 ml
Garlic, crushed	1/2 cup	125 ml
Honey	1/2 cup	125 ml
Chives, 1/2 bunch		
White pepper	1 tsp	5 ml
Dill weed	1/2 tsp.	2 ml

Sweet and Sour Sauce

Fresh pineapple, blended	1 part	1 part
White vinegar	1/5 part	1/5 part
Soya sauce	1/5 part	1/5 part
Ginger	to taste	to taste
Cornstarch		
Water		

Over a low heat, mix together 1 part blended fresh pineapple, 1/5 part white vinegar and 1/5 part soya sauce in a small pot. Add ginger to taste, water and corn starch to thicken.

Phil Pappin, Chef
Grizzly House, Banff

CHICKEN BREAST TICINO

serves four

Chicken breasts, double	4	4
Fresh goat cheese	1 cup	250 ml
Cream cheese	2 cups	500 ml
Green onions, chopped	1/2 cup	125 ml
Egg yolks	2	2
Bread crumbs	1 1/2 cup	375 ml
Hazelnuts, ground	1 1/2 cup	375 ml
Eggs, lightly beaten	2	2
Salt and pepper	to taste	to taste

Clean the chicken breasts (take the skin off), open them to butterfly shape and pound well. Mix goat and cream cheese with chopped green onions and egg yolks. Season the chicken breasts on both sides and spread cheese mixture over one side. Fold the other side over. Mix the bread crumbs with ground hazelnuts, dip the chicken breasts in the eggs and bread them with the mixture. Brown the chicken breasts in a little butter on both sides and bake them in the oven at 350°F(180°C) for approximately 10 to 12 minutes.

Markus Wespi, Chef/Co-owner
Ticino Restaurant, Banff

"Perhaps Mohammed went to the mountain after reading a ... folder about Banff"

Bob Edward's Summer Annual, 1921

▼

PORK TENDERLOIN DIJONNAISE

serves four

Pork tenderloin	22 oz.	640 g
Butter	2 tsp.	10 ml
Oil	2 tsp.	10 ml
Whipping cream	1 cup	250 ml
Dijon mustard, hot	2 tbsp.	30 ml
Sour pickles, small cubes	1	1
Shallots, chopped	1 tbsp.	15 ml
White wine	1/4 cup	50 ml
Salt and pepper	to taste	to taste

Slice pork tenderloin into 12 medallions, spice to taste and roll in flour. In a large frying pan sauté in oil and butter until done. Place medallions on plate and keep warm.

In the same pan sauté shallots then add wine, cream, pickles and mustard. Let simmer for about 2 minutes. Add salt and pepper and pour sauce over the medallions.

Serve with rice or noodles.

Markus Eisenring, Chef/Owner
Peppermill Restaurant, Canmore

"Banff is a playground set midst wondrous beauty, but Lake Louise is Beauty's Shrine...the Mona Lisa of the Mountains."

Banff Crag and Canyon, June 15, 1928

▲

▼

COCONUT CURRY CHICKEN

serves two

Ingredient	Imperial	Metric
Chicken breasts, skinned and boneless	2	2
Madras curry paste (available at Superstore)	2 tbsp.	30 ml
Coconut milk	1/2 cup	125 ml
Port wine	2 tbsp.	30 ml
Peppers, diced - use green, red and yellow	1/3 cup	75 ml
Onion, diced	3 tbsp.	45 ml
Mushrooms, diced	2 tbsp.	30 ml
Tomato sauce, canned	1/4 cup	50 g
Chicken broth	1/3 cup	75 ml
Cilantro, chopped	1 tsp.	5 ml
Coconut, shredded and toasted		
Salt	to taste	to taste
Olive oil	2 tbsp.	30 ml
Fresh lemon	1/2	1/2

Lightly salt chicken and baste with curry paste. Quickly broil or pan fry to seal the chicken. (Chicken should still be pink when sealed). Slice chicken into strips about 1/2 " (12 mm) wide, set aside and keep warm.

In oil, sauté peppers, mushrooms and onions until they are transparent but still crisp. Add port, broth, tomato sauce, remaining curry paste and coconut milk and bring to a boil. Reduce heat and simmer until slightly thick.

▲

▼

Stir in chicken and continue simmering until chicken is cooked, for about 2 minutes. If sauce becomes too thick, more broth may be added.

Just before serving, stir in cilantro and juice of 1/2 lemon.

Serving suggestion: Serve on a bed of white rice and sprinkle with toasted coconut. Garnishes served on the side may include chutney, pineapple pieces, raisins, chopped tomatoes or cucumber and banana slices.

Option: Curry paste can be substituted with quality curry powder - to taste.

Henry Vultier, Executive Chef
Banff Park Lodge, Banff

"You can't enjoy the most entrancing view or even be sociable with your fellow men if your stomach is full of say—burnt beans."

Harold Pripps, quoted by Elon Jessup in "Camp Grub", 1924

▲

▼

EGGPLANT PARMIGIANA

This is a meal in itself! Parmigiana takes time to prepare - like all good things in life! Count on at least 2 hours to prepare this dish. So pour yourself a glass of wine, turn on the music and pursue this culinary adventure! Some standard parmigiana recipes use ricotta cheese. This is a lighter version with low-fat cottage cheese and less salt! Double the portions to make an extra batch for the freezer.

Makes four to six portions

2 small eggplants (each)	1 lb.	250 g
salt for draining eggplants		

Tomato sauce: makes about 3 cups

Olive oil	2 tbsp.	30 ml
Coarsely chopped onions	1 cup	250 ml
Medium carrots, peeled and chopped	3	3
Canned whole tomatoes	14 oz.	454 g
Tomato sauce	14 oz.	454 g
Garlic cloves, chopped	2	2
Fresh or dried basil	1 tbsp.	15 ml
Dried thyme	1 tsp.	5 ml
Cayenne pepper	1/4 tsp.	1 ml
Bay leaf	1	1
Balsamic or apple cider vinegar	1 tbsp.	15 ml.
Fresh ground black pepper	to taste	to taste

▲

▼

Cottage cheese mixture

Low-fat cottage cheese ....1 cup .....250 ml
Eggs ....2............2
Chopped parsley ....1 cup .....250 ml
Grated mozzarella cheese ....4 cups ....1 l
Parmesan cheese...........................1/4 cup ..60 ml

Eggplant preparation: Slice eggplants into 1/4 " (5 mm) rounds (don't peel it). Salt both sides of the rounds generously, laying the slices in a colander. (Eggplant is salted to remove excess moisture, which can be bitter. It also soaks up a great deal of oil when sautéed - salting can reduce oil absorption by two-thirds!) LEAVE SALTED EGGPLANTS TO SWEAT FOR 1 HOUR. You can make the tomato sauce and prepare the other ingredients while the eggplant sweats and drains.

Tomato sauce preparation: Brown the onions in the olive oil. Add the rest of the ingredients. Simmer for 30 minutes. Remove the bay leaf and purée the sauce in your food processor. Double this recipe if you want extra to freeze for spaghetti sauce, lasagne or gnocchi.

Cottage cheese mixture: combine cottage cheese, eggs, parmesan and parsley. Grate 4 cups (1 l) mozzarella cheese.

Back to the eggplant! Drain and rinse the slices 2 to 3 times with cold water to remove all of the salt. Leave slices on paper towels to absorb moisture. Pat dry.

Frying the eggplant: (Pour yourself another glass of wine at this point!)

Heat 2 tbsp. (30 ml) of olive oil in a skillet over medium-high heat for each batch of eggplant to be browned. (I use a measuring spoon to ensure that I don't use too much oil.) Lightly brown eggplant slices on each side. DO NOT ADD MORE OIL WHILE THE EGGPLANT IS COOKING. Remove cooked slices and place on paper towels to drain. Repeat until all eggplant pieces are done.

continued on page 90

▲

▼

Assembling the final product: Spread 1 cup (250 ml) tomato sauce over the bottom of an oval 9" x 12" (23 x 30 cm) gratin dish. Arrange a layer of eggplant slices over the sauce. Top each slice with a spoon of cottage cheese mixture. Sprinkle 1 cup (250 ml) of mozzarella cheese over the layer. Arrange the next layer of eggplant so that it overlaps the first round. Add cottage cheese and mozzarella. After adding the final layer of eggplant and cottage cheese, spoon the remaining tomato sauce over the casserole. Sprinkle with the remaining mozzarella.

Bake in 350°F(180°C) degree oven for 25 - 30 minutes, until the mozzarella is browned and the mixture bubbles. If you have made extra parmigiana, freeze it uncooked. Before baking, unthaw it in your microwave.

Barb Renner, Mt. Assiniboine Cookbook, Mt. Assiniboine Lodge
Mt. Assiniboine Provincial Park

"Dress your duck and allow a slow cook to walk through a hot kitchen with it."

comment on cooking duck rare 1924, Elon Jessup in 'Camp Grub'

▲

▼

FILLET OF SEA BASS WITH FRESH MEDITERRANEAN HERBS & RED PEPPER SAUCE

serves six

Fillet of sea bass (six) each	6 1/2 oz	180 g
Fresh or dried oregano, basil, thyme and marjoram	2 tsp.	10 g
Olive oil	2/3 cup	150 ml
Butter	6 tbsp.	90 ml
Shallots	2 tbsp.	30 ml
Butter	1 tbsp.	15 ml
White wine	1 cup	250 ml
Fish stock	2/3 cup	150 ml
Red pepper, peeled (optional - canned pimentos)	11 oz.	300 g
Salt and pepper	to taste	to taste

Purée red pepper in blender. Season to taste. Sauté the shallots in 1 tbsp. (15 ml) of butter, then add the white wine and the fish stock. Both liquids will reduce to half. Add the red pepper purée.

In a hot pan melt the butter and add olive oil.

Season the fillet of sea bass with salt, pepper and herbs.

Sauté the fillet on each side for 3 to 4 minutes. Remove from pan and keep warm in oven.

Pour some sauce on a warm plate and place the fish on the sauce. Sprinkle with herbs. Garnish with vegetables and rice.

The Kitchen Brigade
Rimrock Resort Hotel, Banff

▲

▼

LAMB LOIN WITH PEAR WILLIAM SAUCE AND ROASTED GARLIC

serves six

Lamb loin, boneless (six) each	5 1/2 oz	160 g
Virgin olive oil	1/3 cup	80 ml
Salt and Pepper	to taste	to taste
Pears (for garnishing)	2	2

Season the meat with salt and pepper. In frying pan heat the oil and fry the lamb loins to your liking between medium-rare and medium-well.

The Sauce

Butter or margarine	3 tbsp.	40 g
Pear, peeled and finely chopped	1	1
Sugar	1/2 tsp.	2 ml
Pear William liqueur	2 tsp.	10 ml
Whipping cream	4/5 cup	200 ml
Demi glaze	1/2 cup	100 ml

Melt the butter over medium heat, sauté the pears and add the sugar. After the sugar is glazed, add the Pear William and flambé the pears. Add the demi glaze and bring to a boil. Simmer for approximately 5 minutes. Lightly blend the sauce and strain.

Add the cream, bring back to a boil and simmer lightly for another 5 minutes.

▲

▼

Roasted garlic

Garlic cloves...................................4...........4
Virgin olive oil ....1/2 cup ..100 ml

Cut the garlic in fine slices (lengthwise). Heat the oil, add the garlic and fry until golden brown. Strain off the oil (use oil to fry the meat).

To serve: Line the plate with the sauce, place the meat in the middle. Garnish each piece with 1/2 poached pear and sprinkle with the roasted garlic. Serve with potatoes and vegetables.

Gerhard Frey, Executive Chef
Mount Royal Hotel, Banff

"Rev. Father Macdonald declares that Ike Mills' racing team is not composed of prohibition dogs as they show a fondness for light whines"

Banff Crag and Canyon, February 7, 1923

▲

▼

BEEF AND VEAL TENDERLOIN WITH MADEIRA SAUCE

serves six

Beef tenderloin, one piece	16 oz.	400 g
Veal tenderloin, one piece	16 oz.	400 g
Oil (olive or vegetable)	1/2 cup	100 ml
Salt and pepper	to taste	to taste

Preheat oven to 375°F(190°C). Season the meat with salt and pepper. Heat the oil in roasting pan, then brown the meat on all sides roasting it to your liking. Ten minutes will give you medium beef and lightly pink veal. Take out of oven and let rest for 5 minutes before carving.

Sauce

Red wine	1/2 cup	100 ml
Veal stock (dark)	1 1/4 cup	300 ml
Madeira	1/4 cup	50 ml
Corn starch	1 tsp.	5 g
(mix with Madeira)		
Salt and pepper	to taste	to taste

In a small pot, heat the red wine and reduce until almost gone. Add the veal stock and simmer for 5 minutes. Add the corn starch mixture and simmer for another 5 minutes. Season with salt and pepper.

Gerhard Frey, Executive Chef
Mount Royal Hotel, Banff

▲

▼

CHICKEN BREAST WITH TARRAGON YOGURT SAUCE

serves four

Chicken breasts ....4............4

Plain yogurt ....4 tbsp.....50 g

Chicken stock............................1/2 cup ..100 ml

White wine ....1/4 cup ..50 ml

Tarragon, salt and pepper...............to taste...to taste

Butter or margarine

In frying pan sauté the chicken breasts until done. Remove and keep warm. Pour white wine in frying pan, then add chicken stock, together bring to a boil.

Lower heat and stir in yogurt, make sure it does not boil again and season. Pour sauce over chicken breasts and serve on rice or noodles.

Jean-Luc Schwendener, Chef
Mount Engadine Lodge, Kananaskis Country

"'I have a profound respect for bacon', remarked a thoughtful citizen...'Did it ever occur to you that we are indebted primarily to bacon for the opening up and development and civilization of this great and glorious West? That without bacon, this grand country, with...all its ...wonderful evidences of progress and prosperity...would probably be a howling wilderness at the present moment?'

The thoughtful citizen paused for a breath.

'You astonish me', said his friend across the table.'"

from the editorial 'Bacon and Civilization', Banff Crag and Canyon, February 18, 1901

▲

▼

CHAR-GRILLED BEEF TENDERLOIN

per serving

Beef tenderloin	5 oz.	150 g
Asiago cheese	1 1/2 oz.	40 g
Spring salad mix	1 1/2 oz.	40 g
Balsamic vinegar	2 tsp.	20 ml
Extra virgin olive oil	1/4 cup	60 ml
Black pepper, ground	to taste	to taste
Salt	to taste	to taste

Parsley, chopped

Coat piece of tenderloin heavily with crushed black pepper corns. Char-grill for 10 to 15 minutes, turning once until rare. Make a vinaigrette by whisking together vinegar and olive oil, season with salt and pepper.

Thinly slice the Asiago cheese and the rare beef tenderloin. In a large serving dish, layer lettuce, beef and Asiago. Drizzle vinaigrette over salad and garnish with chopped parsley and ground pepper.

Substitute for Asiago cheese: Parmesan cheese.

Kevin Dundon, Executive Chef
Lodge at Kananaskis/Hotel Kananaskis, Kananaskis

"To have only a heavy club between one and a ton and a half of charging buffalo is no adequate protection."

Banff Crag and Canyon, July 17, 1931

▲

Mt. Robson
Mt. Robson Provincial Park

▼

VEAL FRANCESCA

serves two

Veal escalopes (leg or loin) (eight)	1 1/2 oz	45 g
Prawns, black tigers, peeled	8	8
Garlic cloves, minced	4	4
Butter	2 tbsp.	50 g
Parsley, chopped	2 tbsp.	30 ml
Green onions, chopped	3 tbsp.	45 ml
Seasoning salt		
Flour, seasoned to coat veal		
Lemon	1	1
Sundried tomatoes, marinated Italian style	8 - 12	8 - 12

Season the veal and coat with flour. Melt butter in a medium skillet until golden brown, add veal. Sauté evenly on each side, then add prawns and garlic. Sauté until prawns start to turn pink and add sundried tomatoes, parsley and green onions, sauté for 1 more minute and serve. Arrange veal on plates and top each piece with the sundried tomatoes. Arrange prawns on top of tomatoes and finish with a squeeze of lemon and the juice left in the pan.

Serve with your favorite garnishings.

Michael Clark, Executive Chef
Sunshine Village, Banff National Park

"...(the old mountain goat) was not cut down in the bloom of his youth; for though 'K' pounded his steaks to jelly on the stones, and boiled and simmered his legs for hours, he failed to be 'chewable' let alone digestible...and no one of that party ever again sighed for goat."

Mary T.S. Schaffer, 1911, in 'Old Indian Trails of the Canadian Rockies"

▲

▼

CHICKEN BREAST WITH ORANGE CORIANDER SAUCE

serves four

Fresh chicken breasts (four) ....6 1/2 oz ...180 g
Olive oil.................................2 tbsp.....25 ml
Salt and pepper ....to taste...to taste
Ground coriander.........................to taste...to taste
Carrots, small diced 1/8" (3 mm) ....2 oz. ......50 g
Celery, small diced 1/8" (3 mm)......2 oz. ......50 g
Red onions, small diced ....2 oz. ......50 g
Garlic clove, crushed and chopped ...1.............1
Fresh orange juice.......................1/2 cup ..100 ml
Saffron threads ....4.............4
Strong chicken stock (instant or fresh)...2 cups ....500 ml
White wine ....1/2 cup ..100 ml
Cold butter, flakes ....1 oz. ......30 g
Cilantro, chopped ....2 tsp.......10 ml

Season the chicken breasts with salt, pepper and coriander. Heat the olive oil in a sauce pan large enough to hold the 4 chicken breasts.

Sear the chicken breasts on all sides on medium heat until golden brown and bake in the oven until done (approximately 20 minutes).

Remove the chicken from the pan and reserve in a warm oven. Add the garlic, onions, carrots and celery to the hot pan and sauté until tender.

▲

▼

Deglaze pan with orange juice and white wine and reduce to one third. Add the chicken stock and saffron threads, simmer until the sauce is reduced by half.

Whisk in the butter, adjust the seasoning and add the cilantro to sauce.

Cut each chicken breast into 4 slices and place on 4 plates. Spoon the sauce over the chicken and on the plate. Garnish with fresh cilantro leaves.

Martin Luthi, Executive Chef
Banff Springs Hotel, Banff

"There is not much to tell of my trip over Pipestone Pass. It was simply the case of a man starting on a seventy-mile snowshoe trip across the mountains to eat his Christmas dinner with his wife and family, and of getting there and eating the dinner, the pleasure being well worth the trip."

Tom Wilson, pioneer Banff guide, 1909, Canadian Alpine Journal

(Author's note: Frostbite injuries from this trip lead to Tom Wilson losing part of several toes on each foot.)

▲

▼

FILLET OF SALMON NATASHA

serves two

Salmon fillets (portions)	2	2
Ripe tomato, diced	1	1
Red onion, fine diced	1 small	1 small
Green onion, chopped	4 tbsp.	60 ml
Parsley, chopped	1 tbsp.	15 ml
Basil, fresh	6 leaves	6 leaves
or paste	1 tbsp.	15 ml
Butter	2 tbsp.	55 g
Seasoning salt	to taste	to taste
Lemon	1	1

**Flour, seasoned with paprika
 to coat salmon pieces**

Melt butter in a medium skillet until golden brown. Season salmon, coat with flour and sauté on each side. Place skillet in a preheated 400°F(200°C) oven for approximately 10 minutes, or until salmon is just barely cooked. Remove salmon from skillet and onto plates.

In left-over juice, sauté onions, parsley, basil and tomato for 1 minute. Top salmon with mixture and finish with a squeeze of lemon.

Serve with rice and fresh vegetables of the season.

Michael Clark, Executive Chef
Sunshine Village, Banff National Park

▲

VEGETARIAN CHILI

serves 8 to 10

Dried millet	3/4 cups	175 ml
Water	1 cup	250 ml
Vegetable oil	2 tbsp.	30 ml
Onion, large diced	1	1
Medium green pepper, diced	1	1
Medium carrots, diced	2	2
Garlic cloves, minced	2	2
Tomato sauce (can)	16 oz.	454 g
Lima beans, cooked (can)	16 oz.	454 g
Kidney beans, cooked (can)	16 oz.	454 g
Corn, frozen	1 cup	250 ml
Jalapeño pepper, minced	1 tbsp.	15 ml
Chili powder	2 tbsp.	30 ml
Tabasco sauce	dash	dash
White pepper	pinch	pinch

Bring water to a boil, add millet and simmer until soft. In a large pot add tomato sauce, lima beans, kidney beans, corn, jalapeño pepper and millet. In a sauce pan sauté onions, carrots, pepper and garlic until tender, then add to large pot.

Season to taste with chili powder, Tabasco sauce and white pepper. Let simmer for 10 minutes.

Rudi Thoni, Chef
Papa Georges Restaurant, Jasper

"Jasper: 'in the mountains', asinee-watsik in Cree, descriptive."

Indian Names for Alberta Communities, Hugh A. Dempsey, 1987

▼

ELK KILMOREY WITH SASKATOON SAUCE

per serving

Elk steak	8 oz.	225 g
Clarified butter	2 tbsp.	30 ml
Saskatoon liqueur	4 tbsp.	60 ml
Shallots	2 tbsp.	30 ml
Saskatoon berries	1/4 cup	50 ml
Game sauce	4 tbsp.	60 ml
Vanilla ice cream	1/4 cup	50 ml
Cream	4 tbsp.	60 ml

Sauté elk steak in clarified butter, medium rare. Remove steak and deglaze pan with Saskatoon liqueur. Add shallots and Saskatoon berries, cook until tender. Add Game sauce. Add ice cream. Finish with cream.

GAME SAUCE

makes 4 cups (900 ml)

Elk bones	1 lb.	500 g
Celery	1/2 stalk	1/2 stalk
Carrots	1	1
Onion	1	1
Tomato paste	2 tbsp.	30 ml
Pepper corns	4	4
Juniper berries	4	4
Water	8 cups	1,8 l
Red wine	6 tbsp.	90 ml
Brandy	1 tsp.	5 ml
Cider vinegar	1 tsp.	5 ml
Salt	to taste	to taste

▲

▼

Brown bones in 450°F(230°C) oven for about 20 minutes. Add diced vegetables and brown 20 minutes more. Let cool for 5 minutes. Put bones and
vegetables in stock pot and drain grease from roasting pan. Add 1 cup (250
ml) of water and stir, scrape all bits and add to stock pot. Add tomato paste
and remaining water or until bones are covered. Let simmer 4 hours then remove bones and vegetables. Add the rest of the ingredients and reduce by
1/2.

Robert Frost, Executive Chef
Kilmorey Lodge, Waterton

*"...she always moved with much grace, this charming waitress...She waltzed in with a
cup of tea, she waltzed out with an empty dish, and some of us got to keeping time
with her motions...we called her 'The Waltzing Waitress'."*

**on dining in Banff, Edward Roper, 1911, in 'By Track and Trail: A
Journey Through Canada'**

▲

▼

MELISSA'S CHICKEN

serves six to eight

Boneless chicken breast (per serving).....1 1

Eggs ....2..........2

Flour

Prepare egg wash by beating eggs in bowl. Lightly flour chicken and then dip completely in the egg wash.

In a hot frying pan, sauté the chicken in vegetable oil until golden brown on both sides.

Sauce, for six to eight servings

Beef Stock OR

  dissolve cubes of beef base

  in 5 cups of boiling water..............5 cups ....1,3 l

Butter..............................4 tbsp.....60 ml

Flour ....4 tbsp.....60 ml

White wine ....1/2 cup ..125 ml

Medium size onion ....1/2 ....1/2

Small tomato ....1..........1

Salt and pepper ....to taste...to taste

Tarragon....................................to taste...to taste

Parsley, as garnish

Slice onion and finely chop tomato and sauté over a medium heat in butter for about 3 minutes. Add flour and stir until smooth. Add a pinch of tarragon and slowly stir in beef stock and white wine. Bring to a boil for about 5 minutes and salt and pepper to taste.

To serve, place chicken on a bed of fluffy white rice and generously cover with sauce. Garnish with a sprig of fresh parsley.

Melissa's Restaurant & Bar, Banff

▼

BAKED SALMON FILLET WITH SESAME CAPER BUTTER

This is a very elegant, yet simple way to serve salmon.

serves four

Salmon fillets ....4............4

Sesame caper butter

Butter..4 tbsp.....60 ml

Green onions, finely chopped ....2 tbsp.....30 ml

Sesame oil......................................1 tsp.......5 ml

Soy sauce ....1 tsp.......5 ml

Capers ....1 tsp.......5 ml

Sesame seeds..................................2 tbsp.....30 ml

Mix butter, green onions, sesame oil, and soy sauce together. Toast sesame seeds in the oven until lightly browned.

Add hot sesame seeds to butter mixture. Stir well. Pour the mixture on a piece of foil or waxed paper and roll into a cylinder. Place in freezer for half an hour.

To cook the salmon fillets: place salmon fillets on a cookie sheet. Preheat the oven. Bake for 15 to 20 minutes. The translucent flesh of the salmon will turn opaque once it is cooked (check by inserting a knife in the thickest part of the fillet). Do not overcook.

Remove sesame butter from the freezer. Slice rounds of frozen butter and place one on each fillet before serving.

Oven 400°F(200°C). Bake 15 to 20 minutes

Microwave 5 to 10 minutes

Barb Renner, Mt. Assiniboine Cookbook, Mt. Assiniboine Lodge
Mt. Assiniboine Provincial Park

▼

CHICKEN ALMONDINE AU CURRY

serves two

Chicken

Chicken breast	2	2
Flour	1/3 cup	80 ml
Large eggs	2	2
Milk	2 tbsp.	30 ml
Sliced almonds	1/2 cup	125 ml
Salt	to taste	to taste
Pepper	to taste	to taste
Butter	1/4 cup	50 ml

Curry sauce

Curry	2 tsp.	10 ml
Small onion	1	1
Banana	1	1
Apple	1/2	1/2
Coconut, dried	1/3 cup	75 ml
Chicken broth	1 cube	1 cube
Water	1 cup	250 ml

Roux

Butter	2 tbsp.	30 ml
Flour	1/4 cup	50 ml

Take the two chicken breasts and season them with salt and pepper. Cover both sides with flour and dip the chicken breasts in egg and cover both sides with sliced almonds.

Warm up a pan until it almost smokes. Put both chicken breasts in it until it is golden brown on both sides. Finish in a 375°F(190°C) preheated oven and cook for approximately 10 minutes.

▲

▼

Coarsely chop onions, banana and apples and pan-fry at moderate heat for 10 minutes. Add curry and coconut and simmer for a couple of minutes. Add water and when boiling add chicken cube, let reduce for 10 minutes. After 10 minute period, strain the stock into another pot, when boiling again add roux to gradually thicken.

To make the roux, melt butter, add flour and stir until well mixed.

To finish, put sauce on the plate and place chicken on top.

Michel Payant, Sous Chef
Chateau Jasper, Jasper

"I am told to consult carefully a food-value list...for the good of my health...Maybe if I did, I'd live to be a hundred...Unfortunately, the camper is too busy to puzzle it out: one has to go fishing."

Elon Jessup, 1924, in 'Camp Grub'

▲

▼

HERB ROASTED CHICKEN WITH FRESH ASPARAGUS AND NEW SPRING POTATOES

serves four

Chicken breast with thigh attached (boneless)	4	4
Fresh rosemary, chopped	1/2 tsp.	2 - 3 g
Fresh thyme, chopped	1/2 tsp.	2 - 3 g
Fresh basil, chopped	1/4 tsp.	1 g
Vegetable oil, as needed		
Fresh ground pepper	to taste	to taste
Salt	to taste	to taste
Flour		

Pull back the skin of the chicken and rub the fresh herbs very generously into the flesh. Pull the skin back in place.

Heat a medium size heavy skillet or electric frying pan. Add the vegetable oil and heat.

If you are using a coated (non stick) pan, then you will have no problem with the skin sticking. If you are using a regular frying pan, then you can coat the breasts with flour just so it is lightly dusted. This will help in both browning the meat as well as keeping the juices locked in.

Brown the breasts in the oil and then season. You will finish them in the oven at 350°F(180°C) for about 10 to 15 minutes.

Serve with fresh lemon, new potatoes and fresh asparagus.

David MacGillivray, Executive Chef
Jasper Park Lodge, Jasper

▲

BEEF STROGANOFF

serves 6 - 8

Alberta beef, well aged	48 oz.	1500 g
Shallots, chopped	5 oz	150 g
Mushrooms, quartered	11 oz	300 g
Sour cream	7 oz.	200 g
Tomatoes, chopped	14 oz	400 g
Cornichons, julienne	16 oz.	450 g
Whipping cream	11 oz.	300 g
Brandy	2 oz.	55 g^

Cut the trimmed beef into 1 1/4 " (3 cm) cubes and season with salt, pepper and paprika.

In a deep frying pan, heat oil and butter and sauté meat, browning rapidly on all sides - keeping it medium rare. Remove from pan and keep warm.

In the same pan, sauté the shallots to a golden brown, stirring continuously with a wooden spoon. Deglaze with the brandy and add quartered mushrooms, stir for a minute and add chopped tomatoes and half the sour cream and lemon juice.

Let the sauce reduce for a few minutes, season and finish with whipping cream.

When the sauce is ready, mix in the beef and 3/4 of the cornichons, do not let the sauce boil once the meat has been added (the meat will become tough).

Serve with rice pilaf and garnish with sour cream and the remaining cornichons on top.

Jaroslav Nydr, Executive Chef
Chateau Lake Louise, Lake Louise

Fenny Fowles in costume, *Byron Harmon photograph*, 1912

Desserts (and Breakfast)

▼

POPPYSEED CAKE

makes two 9" (22 cm) cakes
Cake
Poppyseeds ....1/2 cup ..125 ml
Milk ....3/4 cup ..175 ml
Butter...3/4 cup ..175 ml
Sugar...1 1/4 cup..300 ml
Flour ....2 1/4 cup..550 ml
Baking powder ....2 1/2 tsp...12 ml
Salt ....1/2 tsp ...2 ml
Vanilla ....1 tsp ......5 ml
Egg whites ....4............4

Filling

Sugar...1/2 cup ..125 ml
Corn starch...................................2 tbsp.....30 ml
Milk ....1 cup .....250 ml
Egg yolks ....4............4
Chopped walnuts ....1/2 cup ..125 ml
Vanilla ....1/2 tsp. ..2 ml

Icing

Stiff whipped cream.......................2 cups ....500 ml

Soak poppyseeds and milk together for 30 minutes. Cream together the butter and sugar. Sift together flour, salt and baking powder. Beat egg whites until stiff. Are all your bowls dirty yet?

▲

Cascade Mountain
Banff National Park

▼

Add the vanilla to the poppyseeds and milk, then alternately add with the flour mixture to the butter. Gently fold whipped egg whites into the whole mixture. Divide into 2 greased 9" (22 cm) pans. Bake in a preheated oven at 350°F(180°C) for 25 to 30 minutes.

In a saucepan blend all the filling ingredients together. Bring to a boil, stirring constantly, until smooth and thick then add the nuts and vanilla.

Spread filling between the 2 cakes and ice with the whipped cream.

Skoki Lodge, Banff National Park

Carl Rungius, the great animal painter of New York, was a guest this week at the King Edward. He then went north with Jimmy Simpson as guide. Jimmy will sure lead him into green pastures and beside still waters."

Banff Crag and Canyon, August 4, 1917

KILLER PANCAKES

serves four Neanderthals or six regular appetites

Large eggs at room temperature	3	3
Sour cream	1 cup	250 ml
OR yogurt	3/4 cup	175 ml
OR buttermilk	1 cup	250 ml
Milk	1 cup	250 ml
plus a bit more milk	2 tbsp.	30 ml
All purpose flour	1/2 cup	125 ml
Whole wheat flour	1/2 cup	125 ml
Baking soda	1 tsp.	5 ml
Baking powder	1 1/2 tsp.	7 ml
Sugar	1 tsp.	5 ml
Oil, if not using non-stick pan	1 1/2 tbsp.	22 ml
Blueberries, fresh OR thawed	3/4 cup	300 ml
Butter	to taste	to taste
Maple syrup	to taste	to taste

Separate eggs and set whites aside. Beat yolks and add in the sour cream or yogurt or buttermilk.

Sift together the all-purpose flour, whole wheat flour, baking soda, baking powder and sugar. The whole wheat flour contains wheat germ and this will be left in the sifter. Save a few tablespoons of it to use on the top of the pancake and add the rest to the dry ingredients.

Add dry ingredients slowly to the wet mix. Stir just enough to blend ingredients. Stir in oil if needed.

Using clean beaters, whip egg whites until firm. Fold whites into mixture and just combine.

Pour onto a hot pan (375°F, 190 °C). Immediately place a few blueberries into each pancake Brown on both sides. Serve, spread with butter and sprinkle wheat germ on top. Pour maple syrup over pancakes.

Variations: Substitute other fruits or a mixture of fruits. Can also be used as a waffle batter.

Greg and Neil Ronaasen
Coyote's Deli & Grill, Banff

CLAFOUTI

serves six to ten

Berries, of your choice	1 1/2cups	375 ml
Eggs	4	4
Flour	1 cup	250 ml
Milk	2 cups	500 ml
Sugar	1/2 cup	125 ml
Melted butter	2 tbsp.	30 ml
Vanilla	1 tbsp.	15 ml
Salt	pinch	pinch

Butter, to coat pan

Grease a Clafouti dish (oval and deep) and cover bottom with a layer of frozen or fresh berries.

In a large saucepan mix until warm, the milk, sugar, butter, vanilla and salt. Remove from the heat. With a whisk, slowly add the flour and eggs, stirring constantly.

Pour mixture over the berries and bake in a preheated oven at 400°F(200°C) for 30 to 35 minutes or until set. Serve warm or cold for breakfast or dessert.

Skoki Lodge, Banff National Park

SWEET CHEESE CUSTARD

serves four

Quark cheese ....1 1/4 cup..175 ml

Sugar..1/3 cup ..75 ml

Whipping cream.........................1/2 cup ..125 ml

Small orange, grated peel

Orange liqueur ....1 Tbsp....15 ml

Fresh blueberries ....2 cups ....500 ml

Fresh mint or chocolate shavings......as garnish

Blend cheese and sugar using beaters or a food processor. Add cream, orange peel and liqueur. Arrange fruit and custard in layers in a dessert glass. Garnish with fresh mint or chocolate shavings.

The custard will keep in the refrigerator for as long as the expiry date on the cheese and whipping cream.

Variations: Use any fresh berries - strawberries, raspberries, blackberries, fresh apricots or melons. Can also use a different fruit for each layer.

Mike Derondeau, Owner
Guido's Ristorante, Banff

"Banff during summer weekends is the liveliest place in Alberta."

The Morning Albertan, July 15, 'that's life for me.'"

▼

PEAR WILLIAM FONDUE

Milk .... 1 cup ..... 1/4 l
Sugar .... 4 tbsp. ..... 60 ml
Vanilla bean 1 1
Grated lemon peel .... to taste ... to taste
Cinnamon .... to taste ... to taste
Cloves .... to taste ... to taste
Coriander, ground .... to taste ... to taste
Chocolate pudding .... 1 pouch .. 1 pouch
Whipping cream .... 2/3 cup .. 150 g
Pear William Schnapps .... 1/2 cup .. 125 ml

Dip chunks of Comice Pears and "Lady Fingers" into the chocolate fondue.

Jaroslav Nydr, Executive Chef
Chateau Lake Louise, Lake Louise

"...to give the trail-breakers a welcome, a bright idea popped into my head. They shall have...pudding.' I made the pudding and we all tasted it and it was a good pudding, that is if it had been intended for a cannon-ball...our campsite may fade, our trip forgotten, but that pudding ought to be there when the next explorers go through."

Mary T.S. Schaffer, 1911, in 'Old Indian Trails of the Canadian Rockies'

▲

▼

STRAWBERRIES ROMANOFF

Strawberries	16 oz.	500 g
Grand Marnier or substitute	5 tsp.	25 ml
Sugar	3 1/2 oz.	100 g
Whipped cream	1 1/3 cup	300 g

The strawberries are macerated in liqueur and sugar. They are garnished with whipped cream and additional strawberries.

Jaroslav Nydr, Executive Chef
Chateau Lake Louise, Lake Louise

ROYAL KIR GRANITA

serves four

Fresh black currants	1 cup	250 ml
Sorbet syrup (see below)	1 1/2 cup	375 ml
Champagne or sparkling white wine	1/2 bottle	1/2 bottle

Put black currants and the sorbet syrup in a sauce pan and simmer for 5 minutes. Pass mixture through a fine sieve and let cool. Stir in the champagne and place mixture in the freezer until it forms an icy consistency, stir well and serve in tall parfait glasses. Great for hot summer days.

Sorbet Syrup

Caster sugar	1 1/2 cup	375 ml
Water	2 cup	500 ml

Dissolve the sugar in the water over low heat, then bring to a boil. Set aside and cool.

Variations: Use raspberries, blackberries or blueberries.

Milos J. Moravcik, Executive Chef
Inns of Banff Park, Banff

▲

▼

PEAR TARTE TATIN

serves eight

Pears, peeled, cored and sliced	5 - 6	5 - 6
Butter	4 tbsp.	60 ml
Sugar	1/4 cup	50 ml
Cinnamon	to taste	to taste
Nutmeg	to taste	to taste
Pie pastry, rolled to 12" (31 cm),		
1/8" (3 mm) thick		
Whipping cream, whipped,		
as topping when serving	1 cup	250 ml

On stovetop, in an oven proof skillet, melt butter. Add sugar and caramelize (be careful as sugar burns very easily). Remove from heat. Add pears, sprinkle with cinnamon and nutmeg. Cover with pie pastry and with a paring knife stab through the pastry to vent. Bake 10 minutes in a preheated 400°F(200°C) oven, then reduce heat to 375°F(190°C) and bake for 20 minutes.

Using oven mitts on both hands, remove from oven, invert large platter over skillet, turn skillet and platter over together so that tarte is now on platter, pastry side down. (Watch for hot caramelized sugar that may leak over edges of platter.)

Cut and serve with whipped cream.

Scott Schroeder, Executive Chef
Lake O'Hara Lodge, Yoho National Park

"I am DEE-LIGHTED with your town."

former US President Teddy Roosevelt, visiting Banff in 1915

▲

▼

CHOCOLATE PECAN TARTE

serves twelve to sixteen

Crust

Pecans, coarse ground, roasted ....1 cup .....250 ml
Chocolate wafer crumbs.................1 1/2 cup..375 ml
Cinnamon....................................1/4 tsp. ..2 ml
Nutmeg ....pinch .....pinch
Butter, melted ....2/3 cup ..150 ml
Butter and flour, to coat pan

Filling

Whipping cream...........................2 cups ....450 ml*
Semi-sweet chocolate.....................16 oz. ....500 g
Frangelico or Amaretto liqueur........1/4 cup ..50 ml

Topping

More roasted, crushed pecans
Whipping cream, whipped, on
plate when serving, to taste ....1 cup .....250 ml

Butter and flour bottom of 9" (22 cm) spring form pan.

In a mixing bowl, combine first five ingredients. Press into bottom of prepared pan. Bake in a preheated 350°F(180°C) oven for 8 minutes and cool completely.

Melt chocolate in double boiler. Remove from heat. Heat cream to just boiling. Whisk cream into chocolate until smooth. Stir in liqueur and cool slightly, stirring occasionally.

▲

Pour chocolate mixture into cooled crust and tap gently on counter (removes air bubbles). Sprinkle more roasted, crushed pecans over tarte, and refrigerate overnight.

Serve small portions with whipped cream.

★Note: The usual equivalency for 2 cups is 500 ml. This recipe calls for the more exact conversion of 450 ml. This is to ensure that the filling will set properly. Too much whipped cream will make the filling too soft.

Scott Schroeder, Executive Chef
Lake O'Hara Lodge, Yoho National Park

"To preserve children: Take one large grassy field, one half dozen children, two or three small dogs, a pinch of brook and some pebbles. Mix the children and dogs well together and put them in the field, stirring constantly. Pour the brook over the pebbles and sprinkle the field with flowers. Spread over all a deep blue sky and bake in the hot sun. When brown remove and place in a bath to cool."

Banff Crag and Canyon, June 29, 1928

▼

CARAMEL HAZELNUT PEAR CRUMBLE

serves eight

Caramel

Brown sugar	2/3 cup	175 ml
Corn syrup, dark	1 cup	250 ml
Butter	1/4 cup	50 ml
Whipping cream	1 cup	250 ml

Pears

Ripe pears	4	4
Sugar	1/2 cup	125 ml
Cornstarch	2 tbsp.	30 ml

Crumble

Flour	2 1/3 cup	575 ml
Butter, softened	1 cup	250 ml
Sugar	1 cup	250 ml
Chopped roasted hazelnuts	1 cup	250 ml
Extra-large egg	1	1

In a medium saucepan mix brown sugar, corn syrup and butter. Cook until sugar is dissolved and butter melted. Add cream and cook until 235°F(112°C) on a candy thermometer. Cool until the mixture is still pourable or just buy one packet of Kraft caramels and melt.

Roast hazelnuts on a cookie sheet until brown. Rub them with a clean cloth, skin will come off easily. Put them in a plastic bag and crush them until they are coarsely chopped.

Peel and wedge pears. Mix sugar and cornstarch together. Toss pears into the mixture and let stand.

▲

Put flour, butter, sugar and chopped hazelnuts in a mixing bowl. Mix by hand or in a large mixer with a paddle until it looks like coarse crumbs. Put half of dough into a 10-inch spring form pan. It is a good idea to butter pan and put a piece of wax or parchment paper on the bottom. Drizzle 1/2 cup of caramel sauce over the bottom crust. Assemble pear segments onto caramel. Put 2nd half of dough over pears.

Bake in a preheated 350°F(180°C) oven for 1/2 hour or until crumb crust is nicely golden. (Special tip: put cookie sheet on bottom shelf of oven to collect melted butter seeping out from sides of pan)

Remove from oven, let cool 10 minutes and remove side of pan while it is still hot.

Serve warm or cold with additional caramel sauce and ice cream.

Marguerite Dumont,Pastry Chef
Chateau Jasper, Jasper

"A wise man once said: 'Every one who has health and strength and is able to kick about the things that don't suit them ought to be satisfied.'"

Banff Crag and Canyon, August 29, 1903

▼

CHOCOLATE APRICOT HAZELNUT TORTE

serves eight

Cake

Semi-sweet chocolate squares	5 oz.	140 g
Butter	1/2 cup	125 ml
Icing sugar	1 cup	250 ml
Egg yolks	5	
Vanilla	1 tsp.	5 ml
Egg whites	5	
Flour	1/2 cup	125 ml
Ground hazelnuts	3/4 cup	175 ml

Filling

Milk chocolate	9 oz.	300 g
Whipping cream	1 cup	250 ml
Chopped hazelnuts	1 cup	250 ml

Coating

Dark chocolate	9 oz.	300 g
Whipping cream	1 cup	250 ml
Apricot brandy	2 tbsp.	30 ml
Apricot glaze, recipe follows	3/4 cup	175 ml

Apricot Glaze (can also use apricot jam)

Dried apricots	1 cup	250 ml
Hot water	1 cup	250 ml
Brandy	2 tbsp.	30 ml

Grease and flour an 8" pan, put wax paper on the bottom. Preheat oven to 350°F(180°C).

▲

Melt chocolate in top of double boiler or microwave method, set aside.

Beat butter with 1/2 cup sugar and egg yolks until light and fluffy. Add vanilla and melted chocolate. Beat egg whites with remaining 1/2 cup sugar until stiff peaks form. Fold beaten egg whites into butter mixture with flour and ground hazelnuts.

Bake in oven for 40 to 50 minutes or until skewer is clean. Let cool on a rack.

Cut dried apricots in half and let soak in hot water and brandy. Set aside.

For filling: Heat 1 cup of cream in a small saucepan. Chop milk chocolate into small chunks and add to cream. Stir until all chocolate is melted. Remove from heat and add chopped hazelnuts. Set aside and cool. When filling is cooled and is thick put in mixer and beat until fluffy.

Cut cake in half. In a baking pan lined with plastic wrap add one half of the cake, and cover with apricot pieces and 1/4 cup of heated apricot glaze. Pour chocolate hazelnut filling on top and then put second half of cake on top.

Refrigerate until hard, about 2 hours.

Heat remaining apricot glaze with 1/4 cup of water. Bring to a boil and stir until liquid state. Take cake out of pan and glaze with apricot glaze.

Heat 1 cup of cream for coating. Add chopped dark chocolate, stir until all chocolate is melted, stir until mix is shiny. Remove from heat.

On a cookie sheet place cake and spread coating evenly until it is a smooth finish.

Garnish top of cake with remaining apricot and hazelnut.

Marguerite Dumont, Pastry Chef
Chateau Jasper, Jasper

▼

BUMBLEBERRY PIE

makes two pies

Crust

All purpose flour	5 1/2 cups	1,375 ml
Salt	pinch	pinch
Lard or shortening	1 lb.	454 g
Egg	1	1
White vinegar	1 tbsp.	15 ml
Cold water	1 cup	250 ml

Filling

Frozen raspberries	2 cups	500 ml
Frozen blueberries	2 cups	500 ml
Frozen strawberries	2 cups	500 ml
Rhubarb, chopped	2 cups	500 ml
Cooking apples, chopped	4 cups	1 l
Sugar	2 cups	500 ml
Flour	2/3 cup	150 ml
Lemon juice	2 tbsp.	30 ml
Egg, beaten	1	1
Milk	1 tbsp.	15 ml

Mix flour and salt. Work in the lard until it resembles coarse meal. Whisk the egg, vinegar and water together. Add to the flour a little at a time until the pastry holds together. Wrap in plastic wrap and refrigerate for 1 hour. Roll the dough into two pie bottoms and two lids.

Toss all the filling ingredients together except for the egg and milk. Divide into the two pie shells. Top with pie lids, crimp together. Mix egg and milk together and brush on pie lids. Slit the tops with a paring knife to vent, and bake in a preheated 350°F(180°C) oven for 50 to 60 minutes, until golden brown.

Tom Hayes, Executive Chef
Buffalo Mountain Lodge, Banff

▼

GELATO AL CAFFE TICINO

serves four

Egg yolks	3	3
Eggs, whole	1	1
White sugar	2 oz.	50 g
White wine	1/4 cup	50 ml

Whip ingredients in hot water "bain-marie", then whip over ice water until cold (sabayon consistency).

Whipping cream	1 1/3 cup	300 ml
Liqueur	1/2 cup	100 ml

(Triple sec. 1/2 part
Kaluha 1/4 part
Brandy 1/4 part)

Instant coffee	1 tbsp.	15 ml
Hot water	2 tbsp.	25 ml

Mix liqueurs with coffee diluted in water, combine with whipped cream and incorporate carefully into sabayon mixture. Fill into glasses or cups and freeze.

Markus Wespi, Chef/Co-owner
Ticino Restaurant, Banff

"I put in all my conscience will allow then add a bit more."

on making camp coffee, 1924, Elon Jessup in 'Camp Grub'

▼

APPLE STRUDEL "MOUNT ENGADINE"

serves eight to ten

Phyllo pastry	3 sheets	3 sheets
Apples (medium Red Delicious)	8	8
Sugar	1 oz.	20 g
Rum	1/4 cup	50 ml
Red wine	1/4 cup	50 ml
Lemon juice	2 tbsp.	25 ml
Hazelnuts, ground	2 oz.	50 g
Cinnamon	1 tsp.	5 ml

Peel and dice apples, mix with other ingredients and spread over phyllo pastry. Wrap to a roll, fold ends over and brush with water to keep moist. Wrap with second phyllo pastry layer and moisten again. Repeat with third layer and bake for 20 minutes at 425°F(220°C).

Jean-Luc Schwendener, Chef
Mount Engadine Lodge, Kananaskis Country

The private distiller or moonshiner, call him what you will, was a wise and cautious man and had a habit of burying his surplus stock... along the banks of Whiskey Creek. The liquid joy, no matter how it was distilled, should be almost priceless now...whoever unearths (this) buried treasure should, in common humanity, donate a small portion (a gallon or two) to the editor of this journal - to be used for scientific purposes."

Banff Crag and Canyon, 1916

▲

Peyto Lake
Banff National Park

▼

SPECIAL GALATOBOUREKO

serves ten to twelve

Egg yolks ....6............6
Sugar...1 cup .....250 ml
Simigdali (wheat hearts)..................1 cup .....250 ml
Vanilla OR ....1 tsp.......5 ml
  Rind of 1 lemon, grated
Milk ....6 cup .....1.5 litre
Phyllo..1 lb. ....500 g
Unsalted butter, melted ....1/2 lb.....250 g

Syrup

Sugar...2 cups ....500 ml
Water...1 cup .....250 ml
Juice of 1 lemon

Beat egg yolks and sugar together until well mixed. Add simigdali and mix well. Stir in vanilla. Pour milk into large saucepan, heat until warm. Stir until thickened, stirring constantly. Set aside.

Place half the phyllo sheets in buttered medium-sized pan, brushing every second sheet well with melted butter. Pour in egg yolk mixture. Top with all but 2 of the remaining phyllo sheets. Turn all edges inward. Bake in preheated 350°F(180°)C oven until golden brown. Remove from oven, let cool.

Combine syrup ingredients in saucepan, bring to a boil and boil for 5 to 7 minutes. Pour hot syrup over cold pastry. Cut into diamond-shaped pieces, serve immediately. Keep pastry at room temperature as it tends to harden if refrigerated.

Note: Simigdali is available in health food stores.

Tom and Maria Lambropoulos, Owners
Balkan, The Greek Restaurant, Banff

▲

▼

BANANA RUM CREPES

six to eight crepes

Large eggs	2	2
White sugar	4 tbsp.	60 ml
Flour	1/2 cup	120 ml
Milk	1/2 cup	120 ml

In a bowl, whisk eggs and sugar until frothy. Add the flour and milk. Blend all ingredients to an even smooth consistency.

Cooking Crepes: Preheat a 10" (25 cm) non sticking frying pan on a medium high heat with one tiny drop of oil. When the pan is hot, lift with one hand while pouring in 2 oz (55 g) of crepes batter. When the batter hits the pan, swirl it around so that it thinly and evenly covers the bottom of the pan. Your crepes should cook quickly. When the crepe is dry and colored brown, flip it with a rubber spatula and cook it for 10 to 15 more seconds. Add a tiny drop of oil to the pan before starting each successive crepe. Layer crepes on a plate with wax paper between each one. Cover with Saran wrap and store in the refrigerator.

Note: If your batter doesn't spread easily, when poured into the hot pan, it may be too thick. Whisk in a little milk and try again. Your finished crepes should be thin.

Crepes filling (four servings)

Bananas, sliced	4	4
Butter	2 oz.	55 g
Brown sugar	1/2 cup	125 ml
Dark rum	1/2 cup	125 ml
Water	1/2 cup	125 ml

▲

Melt butter in a 10" (25 cm) pan over medium heat, add the sliced bananas and cook for 2 minutes. Add the sugar, rum and water. Bring to a boil, mixing all the ingredients in the pan. Place the pre-made crepes in the plates. Have the crepe slightly off center, so that when you fold it in half, it's edge is in line with the rim of the plate. Spoon the bananas onto one half of the crepe and fold the outside edge over the filling. Pour the remaining sauce over the crepes and serve with ice cream or whipped cream. For color, garnish with fresh fruit and a mint sprig.

Daniel Martineau, Chef/Partner
Baker Creek Bistro, Lake Louise

"High up on rocky or snowy slopes one may hear, too, a sharp little nasal bleat and, turning, discover a small greyish animal, about the size of a Guinea pig, with rounded ears, short legs and no visible tail, running rabbit-like across the boulders. This is the pika, cony, or little chief hare of the mountains, also called "the haymaker" from his curious habit of storing away dried grasses and plants for his winter food. Sometimes under an overhanging rock there will be found his miniature haystack, a bundle containing perhaps a bushel of well cured vegetation which includes apparently every plant in the neighbourhood."

on Rocky Mountain Pika from "Jasper National Park" by M.B.

▼

CHOCOLATE MOUSSE CAKE

one cake

Chocolate (semi-sweet) ....14 oz. ....400 g

Whipping cream...........................3 cups ....675 ml

Egg whites ....4............4

Gelatine sheets................................6............6

Method: Melt gelatine and fold into the melted chocolate. In separate bowls whip the cream until stiff and also beat egg whites until stiff peaks form.

Fold whipping cream into chocolate then fold egg whites into chocolate/cream mixture.

Place a layer of sponge cakes in a 10" (25 cm) spring form and pour mousse mixture on top. Allow to set. Glaze with following ganache.

Ganache

Chocolate ....14 oz. ....400 g

Whipping cream...........................1 1/2 cup..320 ml

Melt in hot water "bain-marie" and glaze chocolate mousse cake.

Jan Hrabec
Joshua's Restaurant, Banff

"I wish to complain,' said the bride haughtily, 'about that flour you sold me, It was tough.' "Tough, ma'am?' asked the grocer. "Yes tough. I made a pie with it and my husband could hardly cut it.'"

Banff Crag and Canyon, August 24, 1912

▼

BERRIES GRATIN

serves four

Mixed berries	8 oz.	250 g
Sugar	1 tsp.	5 ml
Kirsch	1/4 cup	50 ml
Egg yolks	4	4
Vanilla extract	1 tsp.	5 ml
Sugar	2 tbsp.	30 ml
Kirsch	1/4 cup	50 ml
Whipping cream	2/3 cup	150 ml

In a bowl, marinate berries with 1 tsp. (5 ml) sugar and 1/4 cup (50 ml) Kirsch. Place berries in a gratin form.

Mix egg yolks, sugar, Kirsch and vanilla extract and beat until creamy.

Whip cream and fold in the creamy egg and sugar mixture.

Pour the contents over the berries and bake in oven by 400°F(200°C) for 3 to 4 minutes. Sprinkle with icing sugar and serve with pistachio ice cream.

Markus Eisenring, Chef/Owner
Peppermill Restaurant, Canmore

"Balloon jumping is the newest sport in England. You attach a small balloon to yourself and it makes you so buoyant that you can jump over barns, haystacks, and trees with ease."

Banff Crag and Canyon, May 8, 1925

▲

CARROT CAKE

one 9 x 13" (23 x 33 cm) cake

Crushed, canned pineapple, drained (reserve juice)	1 cup	250 ml
Raisins	1/2 cup	90 g
Carrots, grated and lightly packed	3/4 cup	130 g
Granulated sugar	2 cups	420 g
All purpose flour	2 1/3 cup	310 g
Baking soda	2 tsp.	10 ml
Cinnamon	5 tsp.	25 ml
Allspice	1 tbsp.	15 ml
Nutmeg	2 tsp.	10 ml
Eggs, large	3	3
Oil	1 cup	250 ml
Vanilla	1 1/2 tsp.	7 ml

Grease and flour a 9" x 13" (23 x 33 cm) cake pan. Drain pineapple well, saving the juice. Boil raisins in pineapple juice, drain and set aside. Place pineapple, raisins and carrots in a bowl.

Combine all dry ingredients in mixing bowl, blend in eggs, oil and vanilla. Mixture will be thick.

Add pineapple, carrots and raisins and mix well. Pour mixture into prepared pan and bake at 350°F(180°C) for 30 to 45 minutes.

When cool, cover with cream cheese icing.

▼

Cream Cheese Icing

Cream cheese (do not use soft,
  spreadable cream cheese)................12 oz. ....350 g
Icing sugar.....................................1 cup .....125 g
Butter, melted but not hot..............1/2 cup ..125 g

Blend cream cheese with icing sugar. Add the melted butter and mix very well.

Chris McKercher, Pastry Chef
Banff Park Lodge, Banff

SUNBURST PLUM CAKE

makes one 11" (28 cm) fluted flan pan

Butter or margarine........................3/4 cup ..175 ml
White sugar...................................3/4 cup ..175 ml
Eggs ....4............4
Vanilla ....1 1/2 tsp. ..7 ml
White flour ....1 1/2 cup..375 ml
Baking powder ....1 tsp.......5 ml

Fruit - fresh plums or peaches, sliced in wedges, or one 28 oz. (800 g) tin canned peaches, drained and blotted dry, cut in wedges.

Cream butter and sugar until light. Beat in eggs, one at a time, then add vanilla. Mix flour with baking powder and add to egg mixture. The batter will be quite thick. Spread batter on flan pan. Arrange sliced fruit on top of batter - press in lightly.

Bake at 350°F(180°C) for 25 to 30 minutes. Serve with light cream.

Sandra Howard
Mt. Assiniboine Lodge Cookbook
Mt. Assiniboine Lodge, Mt. Assiniboine Provincial Park

▼

CREME BRULEE

serves ten

Sugar	1 cup	250 g
Milk	4 1/3cups	1 l
Eggs	2	2
Custard powder	2 tbsp.	30 g
Whipping cream	4/5 cup	200 ml

Caramelize sugar in a pan and carefully add 4 cups (900 ml) of milk. Cook for a moment.

In a separate bowl mix eggs, custard powder and remaining 1/3 cup (100 ml) milk together and add to the sugar-milk mixture. Again, cook for a moment and set aside.

After cooling, add whipped cream and serve with cookies.

Sandra Eichenberger
Le Beaujolais, Banff

"The ignorant imbecile who contributed the Banff items to the (Calgary) Albertan of Saturday's issue may be surprised that his identity is well known, and his cowardly remarks regarding the lady members of the Banff Quadrille Club will but intensify the supreme contempt in which he is already held. The editor of this paper will take pleasure in assisting the ladies to administer to this sneaking reptile the only punishment his miserable apology for a soul is capable of appreciating - a good horse-whipping."

Banff Crag and Canyon, February 2, 1901

▼

FRUIT AND BUTTERMILK PANCAKES

makes about 2 dozen pancakes

Buttermilk or yogurt	1 cup	250 ml
Sunflower seed oil	2 tbsp.	30 ml
White sugar	1 tbsp.	15 ml
Eggs	2	2
White flour	1/2 cup	125 ml
Whole wheat flour	1/2 cup	125 ml
Wheat germ	1/4 cup	50 ml
Baking powder	1 tsp.	5 ml
Baking soda	1/2 tsp.	2 ml
Salt	pinch	pinch

Beat first 3 ingredients together. Add second group of ingredients mixing only until thoroughly moistened. If the batter is too thick, add 2 to 3 tbsp. (30 to 45 ml) milk. Gently stir in 1/2 to 1 cup (125 to 250 ml) fresh fruit (grated apple, sliced peaches, bananas or fresh strawberries and sliced banana).

Fry on a hot greased skillet. Serve with yogurt, honey or maple syrup.

Trudi Wagler-Bowman
Mt. Assiniboine Lodge Cookbook
Mt. Assiniboine Lodge, Mt. Assiniboine Provincial Park.

"...the Banff Literary-Dramatic Club...was quite annoyed at certain individuals who persisted in laughing and snickering during the presentation of 'The Riders of the Sea' - a most dramatic play, depicting the morbid customs of the Irish fisher folk..."

Banff Crag and Canyon, April 24, 1923

▲

▼

FRESH FRUIT AND BERRY TIMBALE WITH GRAND MARNIER ICE CREAM

serves six

Heat proof cups	6	6
Bite size sponge cakes	18	18
Sugar syrup	6 tbsp.	90 ml
Puff pastry circles 1/8" (3 mm) thick and 1" (2.5 cm) larger then opening of cup	6	6
Egg, lightly beaten	1	1
Sugar	2 tsp.	10 ml

Mixed fruit and berries of your choice, cut into small pieces

Place 3 sponge cakes in each cup. In a bowl mix the fruit and berries with the sugar syrup and fill the cups with the mixture. Brush one side of the pastry circles with the egg. Place brushed side down on cups and fold the pastry over the edge, sealing cups. Brush the top with remaining egg and sprinkle with the sugar. Bake in preheated oven at 340°F(175C) for approximately 15 minutes, until golden brown.

GRAND MARNIER ICE CREAM

Milk	1 3/4 cup	400 ml
Sugar	1/2 cup	100 g
Egg yolks	4	4
Whipping cream	1/2 cup	120 ml
Grand Marnier	1/4 cup	50 ml

Orange zest, finely chopped from two oranges

▲

▼

Bring milk to a boil. Combine eggs and sugar in a bowl. Slowly add the boiled milk to the egg and sugar mixture, whisking constantly. Return to pot and heat until slightly thickened without boiling. Remove from heat, add the cream, Grand Marnier and the zest. Let cool in refrigerator for 2 hours then freeze in ice cream maker.

To serve: With the timbale fresh out of the oven, serve one scoop of ice cream on the side. At the table, cut off the pastry lid and place the ice cream on top of the fruit.

Gerhard Frey, Executive Chef
Mount Royal Hotel, Banff

"In the true chef's tradition he threw pots and pans around the kitchen, hurled carving knives at helpers ...(in a rage and) Brandishing a large spoon he...vaulted over...the counter - to land...right in the middle of 360 dessert dishes of jello, each topped with whipped cream and one-quarter of a maraschino cherry."

description of 1920's chef Robert, by Bart Robinson, in his 'Banff Springs - The Story of a Hotel', Summerthought Ltd., Banff, 1973

▼

CHOCOLATE DECADENT CAKE

for 9" (23 cm) round spring-form

This dense, flourless cake is really a cross between chocolate mousse and pâte. Delicious and definitely decadent!

Brownie bottom

Butter	2 1/2 oz.	70 g
Sugar	8 oz.	225 g
Honey	2 1/2 oz.	70 g
Eggs, whole	2	2
Whipping cream	2 oz.	50 g
Pastry flour	4 oz.	115 g
Cocoa	1 1/2 oz.	45 g
Pecan pieces	5 oz.	150 g

For brownie bottom, cream butter with sugar and honey. Add eggs, whipping cream, flour and cocoa and mix thoroughly. Stir in pecan pieces.

Butter and flour a 9" (23 cm) spring-form pan and fill with batter. Bake at 350°F (180°C) until set, the crust should be soft but not liquid. Cool.

Mousse

Egg yolks	6	6
Icing sugar	3 oz.	80 g
Belgian chocolate	8 oz.	250 g
Whipped cream	2 1/2 cup	550 ml
Egg whites	3	3
Granulated sugar	2 oz.	50 g
Fresh fruit		

▲

▼

Melt chocolate in double boiler. Whip egg whites with granulated sugar until soft peaks form and refrigerate. Whip yolks with icing sugar to the ribbon stage and add melted chocolate. Scrape mixing bowl frequently so chocolate won't harden on the bowl or you'll have chocolate chips in the mousse. Fold whipped cream into mixture, then fold in egg whites.

Spread mousse over cooled crust and refrigerate or freeze overnight. Unmold and garnish with whipped cream and fresh fruit.

Kevin Dundon, Executive Chef
Lodge at Kananaskis/Kananaskis Hotel, Kananaskis

"It is not the high cost of living that keeps young people from marriage these days, but the cost of high living; when a young man calls on a young lady now...he has to take her out - and feed her!"

Banff Crag and Canyon, March 29, 1928

▼

CASSATTA ICE CREAM

serves eight to ten
1 Loaf pan 4" x 10" x 3"
(10 x 25 x 8 cm) deep

Vanilla ice cream	40 oz.	1.25 l
Belgian chocolate	6 oz.	170 g
Frozen raspberries	1/2 cup	125 ml
Grenadine	2-3 tbsp.	30 ml
Candied fruit peel	3/4 cup	175 ml

1st layer:

Break up chocolate and melt in double boiler. Pour 1/3 of the ice cream into your mixing machine and mix on low speed with the paddle until ice cream is soft. Slowly add melted chocolate while mixing (small chocolate chips will form). Fill loaf pan 1" (2.5 cm) deep with mixture and put into freezer.

2nd layer:

When 1st layer has set repeat step 1, only using raspberries and grenadine.

3rd layer:

Repeat step 1 only using candied fruit peel. Freeze over night before serving and save any left over mixture for next time.

To serve:

Turn loaf pan upside down and run under warm water, using your hand underneath to catch the cassatta as it falls out. Slice desired number of portions (approximately 1" (2.5 cm) thick) and lay on plates. Garnish the plate with fruit slices and whipped cream before serving.

Michael Clark, Executive Chef
Sunshine Village, Banff National Park

▲

▼

MELISSA'S FAMOUS BRAN MUFFINS

yields twelve 7 1/4 oz (210 g) muffins

Bran	3 cups	750 ml
Brown sugar	1 1/4 cup	325 ml
Raisins	2 cups	500 ml
Dates	1 cup	250 ml
Baking powder	1 tbsp.	15 ml
Baking soda	2 tsp.	10 ml
Salt	1 tsp.	5 ml
Cinnamon	2 tbsp.	30 ml
Milk	4 cups	1 l
Eggs	3	3
Vegetable oil	2/3 cup	150 ml
Vanilla extract	1 tsp.	5 ml
Molasses	3 tbsp.	45 ml
Flour	2 cups	500 ml

In a large bowl, combine all dry ingredients. In another bowl, beat milk, eggs, oil and vanilla extract together at medium speed. Add the dry ingredients to the milk mixture, add molasses, and beat for 3 minutes.

Pour the batter into greased chicken pot pie tins (or muffin pans for smaller muffins) and bake at 450°F(230°C) for 30 to 40 minutes or until done.

Melissa's Restaurant & Bar, Banff

"If you don't know why a strawberry short-cake is so called, look for the strawberries."

Banff Crag and Canyon, June 17, 1901

▲

WALNUT GATEAU

one cake

Unsalted butter	3 oz.	85 g
Icing sugar	1 oz.	30 g
Egg yolks	11	11
Walnuts, chopped	7 oz.	200 g
Filberts, ground	2 oz.	55 g
Granulated sugar	5 oz.	140 g
Egg whites	11	11
Ganache (recipe follows)	9 oz.	250 g

Cream together butter and icing sugar very well until creamy. Add egg yolks slowly, creaming continuously until all yolks have been added. NOTE: if mixture looks curdled or split, do not worry.

Whip egg whites and granulated sugar until firm meringue consistency has been reached.

Stir nuts into butter mixture, then carefully fold in the meringue. Pour into a cake ring and bake at 350°F(180°C) for approximately 45 minutes.

After cooled, cut cake through middle. Moisten with alcohol (i.e. Amaretto) optional. Spread thin layer of ganache on bottom half of torte. Replace top. Cover thinly the ganache over entire torte. Place in freezer for approximately 1/2 hour. Take remaining ganache and pour over torte. Cover sides with some chopped walnuts.

Ganache

for 1 torte

Whipping cream............................1 1/4 cup..300 ml

Unsalted butter.............................1 tsp.......5 ml

Dark baker's chocolate

(chopped fine).............................3/4 cup ..175 ml

Bring cream and butter to a boil, then turn off heat. Add chocolate to boiled cream and stir until chocolate has melted.

David MacGillivray, Executive Chef
Jasper Park Lodge, Jasper

"…the proprietor of the bungalow camp at Storm Mountain, 25 miles from Banff…never knows how many lunchers the buses will bring her at noon each day…(so) She has secured carrier pigeons to…carry messages…as to the number of guests…"

The Morning Albertan, July 15, 1925

CHOCOLATE PARADISE

Layers upon layers of chocolate cake separated by a savoury dark chocolate ganache resting on tantalizing Sherry sabayon sauce. Garnish with chocolate sauce and fresh seasonal fruit.

twenty servings

Chocolate	1 lb.	450 g
Eggs	12	12
Sugar	1 cup	250 ml
Salt	pinch	pinch

Preheat oven to 325°F(160 C). Separate the egg yolks from their whites. Combine whites with sugar and whip to make a meringue. Warm yolks and salt in a "bain-marie" (double broiler). Melt chocolate and add to yolk mix. Fold egg yolk mixture and egg whites together. Place in a 18" x 26" (45 x 66 cm) cookie sheet and bake for approximately 15 minutes.

Ganache:

Cream	3 cups	675 ml
Chocolate	2.5 lb.	1.1 kg

Melt chocolate and add cream. Line a 2" x 5" x 10" (5 x 13 x 25 cm) tupperware dish with Saran wrap. Cut cake into layers to fit in pan. Alternate ganache and cake starting and ending with ganache (6 layers of cake and 7 layers of ganache). Wrap cake in Saran wrap and let set in the refrigerator over night.

▼

Sabayon Sauce

Egg yolks 14 14
Sherry ....1 1/2 cup..350 ml
White wine ....2/3 cup..150 ml
Sugar...1 cup .....250 ml

Combine ingredients in a stainless steel bowl and whisk over hot water bath until thick. Cool in refrigerator.

Presenting the finished dessert: Pour 3 tbsp. (45 ml) of sabayon sauce on a decorative plate. Place a 1/2" (12 mm) slice of Chocolate Paradise on sauce in center of plate. Pour lines of chocolate sauce over sabayon. Then using a tooth pick, draw a decorative pattern of your choice. Garnish with fresh seasonal fruit and serve.

Robert Frost, Executive Chef ·
Kilmorey Lodge, Waterton

"While chatting recently with ...the Banff Crag and Canyon editor, he remarked: 'I can give you a good bear story if you like.' 'Well, if its spicy enough.' 'Sure, its about a cinnamon bear.'"

Bob Edward's Summer Annual, 1923

▲

▼

The Banff Springs Hotel, *Byron Harmon photograph,* 1920

▲

▼
RECIPES IN THE CANADIAN ROCKIES

The recipes in this book have been perfected specifically for the high altitudes of the Rockies. When preparing some of these dishes at home, some cooking times will have to be adjusted to your elevation. It should also be remembered that different stoves have varying real temperatures (don't totally trust that dial!). The first time you create one of these delicious tastes of the Canadian Rockies, keep a close watch and fine tune the recipe to your kitchen.

The town of Banff sits at an elevation of 4500 ft (1400 m),Lake Louise (at the lake) is at 5500 ft (1700 m), Canmore is at 4300 ft (1310 m), Waterton is at 4240 ft (1290 m) and Jasper is at 3472 ft (1058 m). The lodges in the back country are at varying elevations. Compared to sea level, at such altitudes water boils at a lower temperature - thus boiling water is actually cooler - and cooking times for processes involving liquids are proportionately longer. A one minute egg at sea level is a two minute egg in Banff (and a four minute egg on the almost 10,000 ft (3000 m) summit of nearby Mt. Rundle, should you happen to be up there for breakfast). In general, when cooking at lower elevations, times for Banff recipes involving liquids should be shortened.

The lower air pressures at higher elevations also mean faster evaporation. Foods cooked in Banff will lose moisture more rapidly that those cooked at sea level; as such, less liquids are required for preparing Banff recipes at lower elevations. As a guideline, decrease liquids by 2 to 3 tablespoons for each cup called for when preparing a Banff recipe at sea level.

Still another effect of lower air pressures is that the gases in baked goods will expand more rapidly than at sea level. To compensate, when preparing Banff baking recipes at sea level, increase baking soda or powder by about 1/4 teaspoon for each teaspoon required, increase sugar by about 2 to 3 tablespoons for each cup called for, beat eggs vigorously, and decrease oven temperatures by about 25°F(15°C). And don't forget to adjust the liquids as well; a moist cake recipe in Banff can become a mush cake recipe at sea level!

A little experimentation will usually be required to create perfect results in your home kitchen. But then, besides the eating, that's the fun part of cooking anyway.

▲

▼

CREDITS

The colour photographs throughout the book are courtesy of the renowned photographer, Douglas Leighton, of Banff, Alberta. A dramatic collection of his work can be found in his bestselling book, *The Canadian Rockies*, Altitude Publishing, 1993. Translated into three languages it makes a great memory to compliment this book!

The historic photograph on page 60 is from the collection of the Glenbow Archives, Calgary, Alberta and is used with their permission. All other historic photographs are from the collection of the Whyte Museum of the Canadian Rockies, Banff, Alberta and are used with their permission.
Edwards, Bob, 'Summer Annuals', 1921, 1923, 1924
Dempsey, Hugh A., 'Indian Names for Alberta Communities', (Calgary: Glenbow Museum, 1987)
Jessup, Elon, 'Camp Grub', (New York: E.P. Dutton and Company, 1924)
Leighton, Douglas, 'A Taste of Banff', (Banff: A Taste of Publishing, 1985)
MacGregor, James G., "Pack Saddles to Tête Jaune Cache" (McClelland and Stewart Limited, 1962)
Robinson, Bart, 'Banff Springs - The Story of a Hotel', (Banff: Summerthought, Limited, 1973)
Roper, Edward, 'By Track and Trail: A Journey Through Canada', (London: W.H. Allen & Co., 1891)
Schaffer, Mary T.S., 'Old Indian Trails of the Canadian Rockies', (New York: The Knickerbocker Press, 1911)
Sladen, Douglas, 'On the Cars and Off', (London: Ward, Lock and Bowden Limited, 1895)
Williams, M.B., 'Jasper National Park', (Department of the Interior, 1928)
'Report of the Rocky Mountain Parks of Canada' by Howard Douglas, Superintendent, (for the years 1903, 1906 and 1911)
'Report of Jasper Park' by R.S. Stronach, acting Superintendent, (yearly report for 1918 - 1919)
'Crag and Canyon', Banff, 1901 - 1931
'Calgary Herald', 1886
'The Morning Albertan', Calgary, 1912, 1925
'Canadian Alpine Journal', Vol. II, No. 1, (Alpine Club of Canada, 1909)

▲

▼

RESTAURANT LISTING

Contributors and their recipes (page numbers in brackets)

Baker Creek Bistro, Banff National Park: Broiled Shrimp with an Asian Sauce(20); Scallop Salad with a Balsamic Vinaigrette(42); Broiled Chicken Breast with a Strawberry Cantaloupe Salsa(81); Banana Rum Crepe(130).

Balkan, The Greek Restaurant, Banff: Delicious Cheese Rolls (Tiropeta)(15); Hearty Moussaka(74); Special Galatoboureko(129).

Banff Park Lodge, Banff: Shanghai Shrimp(24); Coconut Curry Chicken(86); Carrot Cake(134).

Banff Springs Hotel, Banff: Carrot Ginger Soup with Mussels and Scallops(54); Grilled Belgian Endive Salad with Sea Scallops and Roasted Tomato and Garlic Dressing(52); Chicken Breast with Orange Coriander Sauce(98).

Buffalo Mountain Lodge, Banff: Buffalo Satay(14); Parsnip, Honey and Lime Soup(39); Apple Marinated Cornish Game Hen(73); Bumbleberry Pie(126).

Bumper's Beef House Restaurant, Banff: Bumper's Beef Barley Soup(41); Canadian Mountain Stew(78).

Canadian Mountain Holidays, Bugaboo Lodge, BC.: Curry Glazed Pork Chops(80).

Chateau Jasper, Jasper; Tarragon Salad Julienne(34); Chicken Almondine au Curry(106); Caramel Hazelnut Pear Crumble(122); Chocolate Apricot Hazelnut Torte(124).

Chateau Lake Louise, Lake Louise: Beef Stroganoff(109); Pear William Fondue(117); Strawberries Romanoff(118)

Coyote's Deli and Grill, Banff: Cilantro Chili Mayonnaise(16); Green Chili Cilantro Vinaigrette(40); Killer Pancakes(114).

▲

Deer Lodge, Lake Louise: Spinach and Cambozola Cheese Wrapped in Phyllo with Fresh Fruit Salsa(8).

Emerald Lake Lodge, Yoho National Park: Baked Goat Cheese Wrapped in Phyllo Pastry(18); Caribou Loin with Peppercorn Crust(76).

Fiddle River Seafood Company, Jasper: Hot Artichoke Cheddar and Crab Dip(13).

Grizzly House, Banff: Grizzly House Salad(44); Hunter Fondue(82).

Guido's Ristorante, Banff: Basil Sauce - Pesto(63); Sweet Cheese Custard(116).

Inns of Banff Park, Banff: Quesadilla with Hot Italian Sausage and Avocado Salsa(12); Smoked Trout Crostini(10); Exotic Greens, Prosciutto with Lemon Goat Cheese Dressing(38); Fettucine with Tomato Basil Cream(72); Chicken Breast with Goat Cheese and Sundried Tomato Salsa(68); Royal Kir Granita(118).

Jasper Park Lodge, Jasper: Northern Mushroom Soup(55); Buttermilk Baking Powder Biscuits(56); Herb Roasted Chicken with fresh Asparagus and new Spring Potatoes(108); Walnut Gateau(144).

Joshua's Restaurant, Banff: Baked Camembert(22); Mixed Salad with Tarragon Vinegar(43); Mussels with Saffron Sauce(23); Chocolate Mousse Cake(132).

Kilmorey Lodge, Waterton: Okonoki Salad(59); Saskatoon Vinaigrette Dressing(59); Elk Kilmorey with Saskatoon Sauce(102); Game sauce (102); Chocolate Paradise(146); Sabayon Sauce (147).

Lake O'Hara Lodge, Yoho National Park: Garlic Herb Soufflé(11); Raspberry and Balsamic Vinaigrette(33); Spiced Butternut Squash Soup(35); Chilled Fruit Soups (Melon Soup, Berry Soup)(36); Fresh Salmon Spiral with Sundried Tomato Herb Butter(62); Baked Chicken Breast with Fresh Basil and Roasted Garlic(64); Swiss Potatoes(65); Chocolate Pecan Tarte(120); Pear Tarte Tatin(119).

Lake Louise Station Restaurant, Lake Louise: Poppy Seed Lemon Yogurt Dressing(32); Salmon Stuffed Chicken Breast(70).

Le Beaujolais, Banff: Cold Corn Soup with Smoked Salmon(58); Creme Brulee(136).

Lodge at Kananaskis/Hotel Kananaskis, Kananaskis: Veal Tortellini with Shrimp Cream Herb Sauce(27); Tiger Prawns(28); Char-Grilled Beef Tenderloin(96); Chocolate Decadent Cake(140).

Magpie & Stump Restaurant and Cantina, Banff: Queso Sopas (Cheese Soup)(46).

Melissa's Restaurant & Bar, Banff: Melissa's Chicken(104); Melissa's Famous Bran Muffins(143).

Mount Assiniboine Lodge, Mount Assiniboine Provincial Park: Fruit and Buttermilk Pancakes(137); Smoked Gruyere Cheese Salad(48); Eggplant Parmigiana(88); Baked Salmon Fillet with Sesame Caper Butter(105); Sunburst Plum Cake(135).

Mount Engadine Lodge, Kananaskis: Chicken Breast with Tarragon Yogurt Sauce(95); Raspberry Vinaigrette(51); Apple Strudel 'Mount Engadine'(128).

Mount Royal Hotel, Banff: Fresh Scallops with Beet and Red Cabbage Sauce(26); Mushroom Ragout on Four Colors(29); Belgian Endive and Oak Leaf Salad with Pumpkin Dressing(50); Lamb Loin with Pear William Sauce and Roasted Garlic(92); Beef and Veal Tenderloin with Madeira Sauce(94); Fresh Fruit and Berry Timbale with Grand Marnier Ice Cream(138).

Papa Georges, Jasper: Vegetarian Burrito(25); Vegetarian Chili(101).

Peppermill Restaurant, Canmore: Creme de Veau Chasseur(45); Pork Tenderloin "Dijonnaise"(85); Berries Gratin(133).

Rimrock Resort Hotel, Banff: Winter Squash Soup with Scallops(47); Fillet of Sea Bass with fresh Mediterranean Herbs & Red Pepper Sauce(91).

Sherwood House, Canmore: Vegetable Korma(66); Raita(67).

Skoki Lodge, Banff National Park: Skoki Health Bread(17); Stuffed Salmon(77); Clafouti(115); Poppyseed Cake(112).

Sunshine Village Ski & Summer Resort, Banff National Park: Salad Eagles Nest(57); Veal Francesca(97); Fillet of Salmon Natasha(100); Cassatta Ice Cream(142).

Ticino Restaurant, Banff: Ticino Marinated Salmon(19); Chicken Breast Ticino(84); Gelato al Caffe Ticino(127).

INDEX

A Appetizers
B Breakfast
D Desserts
E Entrees
S Soup and Salads

Apple Strudel "Mount Engadine", 128 D
Baked Camembert, 22 A
Baked Goat Cheese Wrapped in
    Phyllo Pastry, 18 A
Banana Rum Crepes, 130 D
Beef and Veal Tenderloin with
    Madeira Sauce, 94 E
Beef Stroganoff, 109 E
Beef Tenderloin, Char-Grilled, 96 E
Berries Gratin, 133 D
Biscuits, Buttermilk Baking Powder,
    56 S
Broiled Shrimp with an Asian Sauce,
    20 A
Bumbleberry Pie, 126 D
Burrito, Vegetarian, 25 A
Butter:
    Tomato Herb Butter, 62 E
    Sesame Caper Butter, 105 E
Caramel Hazelnut Pear Crumble, 122 D
Caribou Loin with Peppercorn Crust
    served with Red Currant Calvados
    Glaze, 76 E
Carrot Cake, 134 D
Chicken:
    Apple Marinated Cornish Game
        Hens, 73 E
    Baked Chicken Breast with Fresh
        Basil and Roasted Garlic, 64 E
    Broiled Chicken Breast with a
        Strawberry Cantaloupe Salsa, 81 E
    Chicken Almondine au Curry, 106 E
    Chicken Breast Ticino, 84 E
    Chicken Breast with Goat Cheese
        and Sundried Tomato Salsa, 68 E
    Chicken Breast with Orange
        Coriander Sauce, 98 E
    Chicken Breast with Tarragon
        Yogurt Sauce, 95 E
    Coconut Curry Chicken, 86 E
    Herb roasted Chicken with Fresh
        Asparagus, 108 E
    Melissa's Chicken, 104 E
    Salmon Stuffed Chicken Breast, 70 E
Chili, Vegetarian, 101 E
Chocolate:
    Chocolate Apricot Hazelnut Torte,
        124 D
    Chocolate Decadent Cake, 140 D
    Chocolate Mousse Cake, 132 D
    Chocolate Paradise, 146 D
    Chocolate Pecan Tarte, 120 D
Clafouti, 115 D
Creme Brulee, 136 D
Delicious Cheese Rolls (Tiropeta), 15 A
Dip, Hot Artichoke, Cheddar and
    Crab, 13 A
Dressing:
    Garlic Dressing, 52 S
    Poppy Seed Lemon Yogurt
        Dressing, 32 S
    Pumpkin Dressing, 50 S
    Saskatoon Vinaigrette Dressing, 59 S
Eggplant Parmigiana, 88 E
Elk Kilmorey with Saskatoon Sauce,
    102 E
Fettucini with Tomato Basil Cream,
    72 E
Fondue:
    Hunter Fondue, 82 E
    Pear William Fondue, 117 D
Fresh Fruit Timbale with Grand
    Marnier Ice Cream, 138 D
Fresh Scallops with Beet and Red
    Cabbage Sauce, 26 A
Garlic Herb Souffle, 11 A

Ice Cream:
  Cassatta Ice Cream, 142 D
  Gelato al Caffe Ticino, 127 D
  Grand Marnier Ice Cream, 138 D
Lamb Loin with Pear William Sauce
  and Roasted Garlic, 92 E
Mayonnaise, Cilantro Chili, 16 A
Moussaka, Hearty, 74 E
Muffins, Melissa's Famous Bran, 143 B
Mushroom Ragout on Four Colors,
  29 A
Mussels with Saffron Sauce, 23 A
Pancakes:
  Fruit and Buttermilk Pancakes, 137 B
  Killer Pancakes, 114 B
Pear Tarte Tatin, 119 D
Pesto Basil Sauce, 63 E
Poppyseed Cake, 112 D
Pork Chops, Curry Glazed, 80 E
Pork Tenderloin Dijonnaise, 85 E
Quesadilla with Hot Italian Sausage
  and Avocado Salsa, 12 A
Raita, 67 E
Royal Kir Granita, 118 D
Salads:
  Belgian Endive and Oak Leaf Salad
    with Pumpkin Dressing, 50 S
  Exotic Greens, Proscuitto with
    Lemon Goat Cheese Dressing, 38 S
  Grilled Belgian Endive Salad with
    Sea Scallops and Roasted Tomato
    and Garlic Dressing, 52 S
  Grizzly House Salad, 44 S
  Mixed Salad with Tarragon Vinegar,
    43 S
  Okonoki Salad with Saskatoon
    Vinaigrette Dressing, 59 S
  Salad Eagles Nest, 57 S
  Scallop Salad with a Balsamic
    Vinaigrette, 42 S
  Smoked Gruyere Cheese Salad, 48 S
  Tarragon Salad Julienne, 34 S
Salmon:

Baked Salmon Fillet with Sesame
  Caper Butter, 105 E
Cold Corn Soup with Smoked
  Salmon, 58 S
Fillet of Salmon Natasha, 100 E
Fresh Salmon Spiral with Sundried
  Tomato Herb Butter, 62 E
Stuffed Salmon, 77 E
Salmon Stuffed Chicken Breast, 70 E
Ticino Marinated Salmon, 19 A
Salsa:
  Avocado Salsa, 12 A
  Fresh Fruit Salsa, 9 A
  Strawberry Cataloupe Salsa, 81 E
  Sundried Tomato Salsa, 69 E
Satay Buffalo, 14 A
Sauces:
  Asian Sauce, 20 A
  Basil Sauce, 63 E
  Beet and Red Cabbage Sauce, 26 A
  Bourgiugnonne (Hot) Sauce, 82 E
  Cream Sauce, 75 E
  Game Sauce, 102 E
  Honey Garlic, 83 E
  Madeira Sauce, 94 E
  Meat Sauce, 74 E
  Mediterranean Herbs & Red Pepper
    Sauce, 91 E
  Mustard Horseradish, 82 E
  Onion Sauce, 82 E
  Orange Coriander Sauce, 98 E
  Pear William Sauce, 92 E
  Sabayon Sauce, 147 D
  Saffron Sauce, 23 A
  Saskatoon Sauce, 102 E
  Sweet and Sour Sauce, 83 E
  Tarragon Yoghurt Sauce, 95 E
  Tomato Basil Cream, 72 E
Sea Bass, Fillet of, with Fresh
  Mediterranean Herbs & Red Pepper
  Sauce, 91 E
Shanghai Shrimp, 24 A
Skoki Health Bread, 17 A

▲

▼

Smoked Trout Crostini, 10 A

Soups:
  Berry Soup, 36 S
  Bumper's Beef Barley Soup, 41 S
  Carrot Ginger Soup With Mussels
    and Scallops, 54 S
  Cold Corn Soup with Smoked
    Salmon, 58 S
  Creme de Veau Chasseur, 45 S
  Melon Soup, 36 S
  Northern Mushroom Soup, 55 S
  Parsnip, Honey and Lime Soup, 39 S
  Queso Sopas (Cheese Soup), 46 S
  Spiced Butternut Squash Soup, 35 S
  Winter Squash Soup with Scallops,
    47 S
Special Galatoboureko, 129 D
Spinach and Cambozola Cheese
  Wrapped in Phyllo with Fresh Fruit
  Salsa, 8 A
Stew, Canadian Mountain, 78 E
Strawberries Romanoff, 118 D
Sunburst Plum Cake, 135 D
Sweet Cheese Custard, 116 D
Swiss Potatoes, 65 E
Tiger Prawns, 28 A
Tiropeta, 15 A
Veal Francesca, 97
Veal Tortellini with Shrimp Cream
  Herb Sauce, 27 A
Vegetable Korma, 66 E
Vinaigrettes:
  Green Chili Cilantro Vinaigrette, 40 S
  Raspberry and Balsamic Vinaigrette,
    33 A
  Raspberry Vinaigrette, 51 S
  Saskatoon Vinaigrette, 59 S
Walnut Gateau, 144 D

▲